THE Dollar Code

Get Out of Debt
With One Number

JASON R. HASTIE

Health Communications, Inc.
Deerfield Beach, Florida

www.hcibooks.com

Library of Congress Cataloging-in-Publication Data
is available through the Library of Congress

© 2014 Jason R. Hastie

ISBN-13: 978-07573-1831-3 (Paperback)
ISBN-10: 07573-1831-2 (Paperback)
ISBN-13: 978-07573-1832-0 (ePub)
ISBN-10: 07573-1832-0 (ePub)

Publisher: Health Communications, Inc.
3201 S.W. 15th Street
Deerfield Beach, FL 33442–8190

Cover design by Larissa Hise Henoch
Interior design and formatting by Lawna Patterson Oldfield

I dedicate this book to my parents, Jerry and Paulette, who taught me about hard work and the value of a dollar. We didn't have much growing up, but we always had enough.

I also dedicate this book to those of you who have struggled with your finances. Maybe you have struggled for a few months, or maybe you have struggled all of your life. I personally and wholeheartedly believe that this book can change your life.

CONTENTS

INTRODUCTION

From Humble Beginnings to Modest Wealth

E very once in a while, a brilliant idea is born out of necessity. Nearly every great inventor who has introduced a new concept did so because of an underlying need that could not be met by an existing means. Therefore, the invention was, in essence, a solution. That is the very epitome of invention.

The same holds true for brilliant concepts. And that is exactly what this book is about. *The Dollar Code* is a concept, stemming from the fundamental principle of budgeting. In today's fast-paced world, too many people have not learned this principle. Maybe you are one of them. Maybe that is why you picked up this book.

The concept of budgeting can be very confusing to people. Even the most educated and intelligent people can get caught up in the momentum of society's expectations. Check-cashing stores encourage borrowing against future paychecks ("paycheques," as they're known in Canada). Credit card companies encourage spending now and paying later. Clever marketing ploys encourage impulse buying. Car dealerships and furniture stores advertise *"Buy Now . . . Pay Later."* Even the whole concept of mortgages encourages debt. Living outside your means has become an accepted way of living. Admittedly, it is very difficult to stay on a budget amidst a world with a *"want it now"* mentality.

So in theory, if you are having money problems, it may not be entirely your fault. Society advocates overspending. Every business has its hand out, just waiting to snatch your pocketbook or wallet. How freely you allow this to happen is entirely a mind-set. For many, overspending becomes a natural way of living.

We all know people who are worse off than we are. People who live paycheck to paycheck—perhaps even you. They get paid on Friday, and by the end of the weekend their money has disappeared. After paying rent and a few bills, they head to the local tavern and blow whatever few dollars they have left. This is a setup for struggling through the rest of the week just to get by, only to start all over again the next Friday.

I have been on "both sides of the coin," so to speak. I know what it's like to feel out of control of my spending and my finances, and I know what it's like *to be in control.* Trust me, it's much better to have that sense of calm that comes with control, especially when it comes to your finances.

I am a Chartered Professional Accountant (CPA)—in the United States, I would be a Certified Public Accountant—and I've owned a consulting practice for many years now. Because of this, you may think that I've always been good with numbers and with controlling my finances. However, it took learning many lessons along the way to bring me to where I am today. One of those lessons came while I was in college. I took a job at Wendy's (the fast-food restaurant), where I first learned about making and spending money. Employees were allowed a half hour lunch break if we worked a minimum of six hours. During that break, most of us would eat Wendy's food. It was good food *and* we got 50 percent off. I thought that was great and took advantage of my discounted lunches for months, until I noticed one very important thing: The meal that I typically ordered (a single burger combo), even at half price, cost me an *hour's wages*! And, to think that I had started doing this every day! Talk about a bad way to spend money.

What I'm going to share with you is a completely different way of handling your finances. *The Dollar Code* takes into consideration the soundest principles of good financial management and budgeting and forces you to look at your finances from a whole new perspective. Let me reassure you—once you learn how to apply the Dollar Code principle to your own life, your financial management will become *super easy* and *very simple* to do. Did I mention easy and simple?

I have read a lot of budget management and finance books. Because of the nature of my business as an accountant, I like to learn new ideas from other respected authors and financial moguls. What I must say is that many of the books, although well written, are just downright complicated. They have complicated formulas to learn, charts to keep, or systems to implement. If a budget is too complex or has too many things to remember, it is just too tough to maintain.

The Dollar Code has none of these traits. It gives you just one number to remember and apply to your everyday living. *One number!* Once you see how easy it is, you will wonder why even the most talented and brilliant financial gurus had never thought of this before. I have found that keeping it simple and adding an element of *fun* makes all the difference.

Then, just maybe, you will feel less stressed. Maybe you will become less frazzled trying to come up with enough money to prevent your electricity from being cut off. Maybe you will be able to have more fun instead of wishing you could afford to do the things you've always longed to do but never could because of lack of money. Maybe you will feel more in control and less worried. Maybe . . . just maybe . . . you can take charge of your life without always feeling pressured, stressed, or unbalanced. After all, you should be in control of your money, rather than allowing your money to control you.

1 The Dollar Code Epiphany

L ife as a kid can be pretty great. The world is open to you, and your dreams are as big as a prairie sky. Like many kids, I wanted music to be a big part of my life. I also dreamed of being a doctor, a lawyer, and all the standard stuff kids think of. Very few kids probably say, *"I want to be an accountant when I grow up!"*

I was raised on a farm just outside a small town in Saskatchewan, Canada, called Birsay. The school I attended was in another town fifteen minutes away, called Lucky Lake. Growing up on a farm was awesome. With the fresh air, open space, and serene surroundings, I was able to develop a vivid imagination. I loved it. I rode horses and motorcycles, and spent my days exploring. It was also a struggle at times, and I saw my parents go through many seasons involving drought, hail, low wheat prices, and low cattle prices. Although there is a lot of pride in farming and working on the land, there is also a lot of risk. Farmers not only have to worry about the weather, they also have no control over selling prices because wheat and cattle are commodities. I did not grow up rich, but I grew up happy. Yet even from early childhood, I remember money always being an issue within our household.

Even as a youth, I knew that I always liked business. Looking back, I can't remember the defining moment that caused me to pursue a degree in accounting, but I guess it had to do with the love of business and the business world. At the time, I think the aspect of working in an office seemed cool.

However, the idea for the Dollar Code was not originally designed as a book or a smartphone application. Just as I explained in the Introduction, the idea was derived out of basic necessity. It was something I did for myself while living in Edinburgh, Scotland, during the summer of 1997.

Six months prior to that, I had attended a seminar for a program called SWAP (Students Working Abroad Program). SWAP allowed university students to work in the United Kingdom while traveling.

Having a working holiday permit gave me the opportunity to travel overseas for the first time, while working to pay for the "holiday," as Canadians and Brits call it (in the US, it's called a "vacation"). While there for the entire summer, I knew that I would have to stay on a very strict budget, especially if I wanted to do any traveling within the UK or the rest of Europe. After securing my first job and a place to live, I assessed *how much money I would need* and *how much I had to have on hand* to live on. Although I had budgeted before, my goal this time was to keep it *really simple*. From this one basic requirement the Dollar Code was born.

Once I learned and applied the Dollar Code, it became an instant transformation in my own mind-set. It became a new way of thinking and looking at the things I bought. It was the "light-bulb moment" of clarity that carried me through my sojourn in Scotland.

I began incorporating the Dollar Code as part of my everyday living, just like putting on socks every day or parking in the same spot at work. It became habitual. It was natural. I didn't ever think of not using it once I had discovered how simple it was. The amazing side effect was that, not only did I remain within my budget, I was actually able to *save* some money, too.

Years later, when my sister came to me for financial advice, I told her about the Dollar Code and immediately recommended it for her situation. She had run into a financial crisis, just as almost everyone does at some point in his or her life. I came to the rescue by applying the same principles I had used myself in Scotland. The realization of how much she spent monthly got her thinking about the impact of the Dollar Code, and she was blown away by the simplicity of how easy it was to use.

After that, I began helping more and more people who were in a financial pickle. Every time I told someone else about it, the reaction was the same: initial surprise and inquisitiveness. So I began using it on my clients within my consulting company. Some were employees, some were business owners, and some were doctors, architects, engineers, local celebrities. All were captivated by the initial concept and the realization of the impact of their daily allowance.

DOLLAR CODE **TIP #1**

"Having a system that is easy to use and easy to remember will help you stick to that system."

2 The Dollar Code and Budgeting

Why Do We Have So Much Trouble Budgeting?

Back in the Old World before currency was the mainstay, when a man wanted goods, he would make a trade. He could trade furs, wood, food, seeds, animals, or many other things. There was no way for debt to occur. The trader stayed within his means. If he did not have any items to exchange, he had to search for alternative means to acquire the things he wanted. He would hunt or fish. He would chop wood. Or he would go without. Either way, he did not have to worry about losing his house or any valuable possessions because they were his. He owned them outright.

The mentality of today's society is to "have it now." People don't want to wait for things they wish to have. The pioneer of plastic (aka—credit cards) was a gentleman named Frank McNamara, who in 1949 went out to dinner and forgot his wallet. To avoid doing dishes to cover his tab, Frank talked his way out of his dilemma by signing for his dinner with a promise to pay it back later. This led to his big idea, and in 1950, Frank and a partner founded Diners Club cards. The cards were first presented by twenty-seven various New York City restaurants to two hundred select individuals. The card allowed the diners to eat and leave with the same amount of cash they came in with. Hence, the modern day credit cards were born.

Plastic has now become a way to *"have it now"* and *"pay it later."* What this has done is separated ourselves from actual money. We see credit as free money. It is not. A perfect example of this is what happened when my sister got her first credit card. I remember her exclaiming to me that she had $500 she could spend (her credit limit). Yes, it is true that she could spend $500. The clincher to this, however, is that if she spent her credit limit, she would have to pay back that $500 from future earnings. So . . . it is not free.

To this day, the widespread occurrence of bankruptcies due to credit card abuse is a main contributor to the decline of many big banks. It also plays a large part in the millions of people who have suffered financial crisis due to overspending on their charge accounts because they have been unable to pay back the borrowed totals. The money-hungry banks charge steep penalties, late fees, over-the-limit fees, and high interest rates. Consumers are at their mercy. The consequences have put many families in a state of dire quandary.

Perhaps you are one of these people. I have met people who have six or more credit cards, including individual department store cards, gas cards, Visas and MasterCards, Discover, American Express—every kind of credit card you can imagine. Stores dangle incentives to save 10 to 20 percent off their purchases to sign up. It's very shady how this all works because once you've bitten the hook, they will reel you in. The plastic and promise to pay later is very tempting.

What School and Jobs Don't Teach You

Our lives are complicated, and budgeting usually only makes it more complicated. When we are young, we learn so much about history, math, language, and science. Why then are we never taught how to take care of a major thing that we deal with *daily* in our adult lives . . . *money*?

For the most part, we learn these lessons on our own. We get conned out of money, and we eventually learn the pain of losing it. We learn the value of money when we buy something that ends up being worthless or that breaks, or something that is intangible (like a much-needed vacation with your family). Only after the money is spent do we feel the pain of our frivolous spending. Even worse, we are given access to money that has not yet been earned (this is called *credit*); we keep spending freely, often becoming prey to the temptations of the various forms of credit. Yikes!

Our mind-set changes to the "having it now and paying for it later" mentality. This is a costly mistake that has led to the breakdown of the global financial system. Rather than merely affecting individuals who are borrowing against future earnings, now the entire banking system, big governments, and whole countries are doing this. It is a volcano that is waiting to explode, with its hot lava hitting the pavement in every city around the world.

What if everyone learned about the Dollar Code? What if everyone started spending only what they had, rather than borrowing against unforeseen and often intangible assets?

You can help me spread the word. You can share the Dollar Code with your friends, colleagues, Facebook buddies, kids, or anyone who will listen. You need to because schools, for the most part, do not teach the essential characteristics of day-to-day living with money.

Yes, school may make kids smarter, but their programs lack in teaching kids about money before they become adults. Teenagers can get credit cards, student loans, or personal loans as soon as they turn eighteen. This is where it all begins: the new lifestyle of living large. Often the consequences carry forward long into adulthood into the late twenties, thirties, forties, and beyond. The once-frivolous teenager then falls into the trap of society's marketing scam. And although that teenager grows up, gets a job, and starts earning money, it is rare to find a company that teaches its workers about spending money. Some adults never bounce back, and they spend their remaining years backpeddling or settling for monotonous jobs just to pay the bills, a direct result of the spending mistakes made early on.

It is much like the analogy used in Robert Kiyosaki's book *Rich Dad, Poor Dad*; the author uses a narrator through the voice of a child who has a poor biological father and wealthy stepfather. The "poor" dad is one who lives paycheck to paycheck and who is helplessly caught in the vicious circle of not pursuing his dreams due to lack of financial ability, even though he was well educated. By contrast, the "rich" dad is a go-getter and has a business mind-set. Therefore, he is able to grasp the concept of not only making money but making more of it by working smarter, not by toiling through a miserable job and existence.

I can tell you firsthand that this is true. I took accounting in high school and then in college. I also received my master's degree in accounting at the University of Saskatchewan, with a BA in commerce. I then became a Chartered Professional Accountant (CPA), known as a Certified Public Accountant in the United States, having interned for three years at an accounting firm. For the last ten years, I have owned my consulting company.

However, in all of those years of school and college, as crazy as it is, I don't remember anyone teaching the concept of handling per-sonal financial matters. Students are simply not educated enough these days in the practical functions of everyday living. It is left to the parents, but many parents have financial problems of their own. They may be the last people who should be teaching a young-ster how to balance a checkbook or prevent bank charges. There is a problem worldwide because the system keeps getting more and more out of hand, much like the proverbial snowball effect.

Actually, it's not entirely the parents' fault. When kids become adults, they still have the paycheck to paycheck mentality that they may have experienced a lot during those years growing up. Raising a family isn't easy, and many parents struggle so they can provide the best for their children. It is human nature, and we are inundated with marketing and advertisements that make us want things. It's easy for a parent to say, *"Let's just charge it!"* and *"My kids need it!"* and worry about it later.

DOLLAR CODE **TIP #2**

"Kids learn about spending habits from parents because personal financial responsibility is not something taught in school. If you live in debt, your kids are likely to follow suit."

Why the Dollar Code Will Help You

The next stage of my epiphany is where you happen to be right now, reading this book. I realized it was my call of duty to help people! By telling everyone I knew (or had just met), I felt like I was helping them out of a miserable situation. Who knows how deep some of them were in before they learned about the Dollar Code? Trust me; it is not too late for you!

I've seen many family members, friends, and clients struggle with their finances, and I know the burden that it places on them. I would consider many of these people to be very smart. So why then are they not smart with their money? Obviously, there are many factors that come into play, but I believe the biggest reason people fail with money is that society—including our parents—never really teaches people *how* to be smart with money. Because of this, we fall prey to many schemes, marketing gimmicks, and ploys by businesses whose goal is to get us to spend more money.

A good friend once gave me some words of advice, which have stuck with me to this day: "*You can only control what you understand.*" If you want to control your finances, save money, and get out of debt, you need first to understand *when* and *how much* you are spending. This is where the Dollar Code can help you; the Dollar Code will help you break down your spending in an incredibly easy, understandable way. This is how the Dollar Code will help you get out of debt and, yes, achieve financial freedom, too, even if other methods in the past have failed you.

Who Needs the Dollar Code?

It doesn't matter how rich or poor your parents were when you were growing up; or how nice a job you have; or how talented, smart, or good-looking you may be. Anyone can become a slave to money.

Do *any* of the statements below apply to you?

- I can't understand *why* I don't have enough money at the end of the week or month.
- I have tried budgeting and *failed* because it was too complicated.
- I feel *out of control* of my finances.
- I get *depressed* about not having enough money.
- I have too much *debt* and feel like the world is caving in.
- I feel constantly *bombarded* by unexpected fees and expenses.

If any of those statements apply to you, then you need the Dollar Code. The Dollar Code will help you "unlock *your* number." It will generate a daily amount for you to live by. In the Dollar Code world, we call this your "*Daily Allowance.*" It's the *one* number you use daily to help you achieve financial freedom. Really . . . it's that simple. And, it's kind of fun, too!

3 What Exactly *Is* the Dollar Code?

As a child, perhaps you were one of the fortunate kids who got a weekly allowance. Whether you had to earn it by shoveling snow off the front step or taking out the garbage every week or whether it was given to you as a treat that you looked forward to, an allowance was more than just about the money your parents gave you to spend on whatever you wanted. It was also a *lesson* in buying and saving.

There were those kids who spent all of their allowance the first day. They ran to the neighborhood convenience store and couldn't wait to pick up fistfuls of gummy bears, eating most of them on the way home. Wasteful and impulsive? Yes. But no different than the adults who spend most of their paychecks at the local pub. As children, many of us "live in the moment" and make purchase decisions based on impulse. Unfortunately, some of those kids carry on these same tendencies into adulthood. After the weekly paycheck comes, the money is often spent by the end of the weekend. Some people pay a few bills and spend the rest on going out all weekend. Others go shopping or spend money on salon services. Either way, it's no fun to struggle for the rest of the week, just waiting for next Friday's payday to come so the same bad habit can be repeated all over again.

DOLLAR CODE **TIP #3**

"Being an adult who spends on impulse is no different from being a kid who gets a weekly allowance and then spends it all at once on candy or toys. Both are examples of financial mismanagement."

Then there were those kids who learned to *save* their allowances, maybe for a bigger toy or something that would give them more gratification than a quick sugary snack. They were disciplined and only bought the big toy once they had enough money saved up. Sometimes, a funny thing happened. After time went by, the kids sometimes changed their minds about wanting to buy the toy. Maybe something different or new caught their eyes, or maybe once they realized how much money they had saved, the desire for that big toy took a backseat to the value they had realized in saving.

The Dollar Code is based on the principle of living within your means. But *what makes the Dollar Code* different *is that it gives you just* one *number to remember:* your *Daily Allowance* (I call this your "DA" for short). This one number is the key to your financial freedom because it makes spending *easy to understand.* Because you understand your spending, you can control it.

Why Just *One* Number?

These days, we all have too many things to remember: usernames and passwords to multiple accounts, dates of upcoming events, bills to pay, phone numbers, locker combinations, codes, birthdays, and countless other things. To some, budgeting seems daunting. It is often pushed to the back burner among the many other hundreds of more important things that take precedence. So I've made it easy.

The biggest advantage of the Dollar Code, aside from how effective it is in your life and your budgeting, is its *simplicity.* You will have only one number to use *every day.* Again, this is your Daily Allowance, or "DA." This is the one number that will, each and every day, get you closer to financial freedom. Because it is the *same* number each day, it is easy to use and easy to remember. It will become engrained in your head, and soon you will be using it without even thinking.

Right now you may be asking questions like:

- ◆ What does this number mean?
- ◆ How do I calculate this number?
- ◆ How do I use this number?
- ◆ Does this number *ever* change?

Let's answer these questions . . .

What Your Number Means

The Dollar Code unlocks your number—*yours!* It will be a number that is unique to you, your income, and your spending habits. And . . . it is the number that will keep you aware and accountable of how you use your money. Ultimately, it is the number that will drive your *success* in understanding and gaining control of your spending, saving for your future, and removing the stress of not knowing where your money is going. You might even say that your number is sacred!

> To explain it simply: *Your number* is the amount of money you can *freely* spend each day without going into debt.

Yes, it's that simple. Now, tell me . . . how liberating is that? How nice would it be to know that you have a daily spending amount that you can use in whatever way you see fit—one that you do not have to feel guilty about or answer to anyone?

Maybe that seems a bit scary to you, too. Chances are, the Daily Allowance (DA) number your Dollar Code unlocks might be quite low. But you're here now. You've picked up this book for a reason. You want to gain control over your spending.

First of all, it should come as somewhat of a relief that you don't have to part with anything you don't want to. Some people swear by their morning cup of fancy java, and that's perfectly okay. Just keep in mind that *everything* will become part of your Dollar Code, so start deducting all daily items you spend money on from your DA beginning with that early morning jumbo Grande-Swahili-Nut cappuccino with cream and Splenda.

The Dollar Code is not about giving up the things you want. It's about staying within your budget and living within your means. One of the *best* lessons it teaches is that of relevance. It will help you understand just how much things you buy *really* cost. I'm going to show you how this all can be done with a simple, yet brilliant, method.

How the Dollar Code Differs from Other Budgeting Systems

Budgeting should not be difficult. Nor should it take a lot of time to set up or maintain. Yet it is. People like you and me have a tough enough time setting up a budget and find it even more challenging to stick to it. Plus, budgeting tends to be an uninteresting chore that is strongly disliked.

I looked at a lot of factors and analyzed why I couldn't stick to budgets in the past. I also questioned some of my clients and friends, asking them why they found budgeting so difficult. The answer I discovered was that it was just too hard to keep track of the numbers in your head. Our brains are pretty incredible, but we are so busy doing those daily tasks of remembering, planning, fretting, and organizing that it's just too tedious to keep track of yet another thing. The only alternative is to write everything down on a spreadsheet.

The Dollar Code is designed to be simple. It is designed to be something that you can stick with. It is designed to be something that you can succeed with.

Almost every other budgeting system that you come across tells you how to set up a *monthly* budget. That sounds pretty standard, doesn't it? Well, let's take a second look. Even though a month may not seem like that long; in reality, it is just plain difficult to do things one month at a time. Most people live in the present. They live in *today*.

Now, let's put this in perspective. As an example, let's say you want to lose ten pounds. You set a goal. What would you do next to try to reach that goal? You may have two things in mind: *exercise more* and *eat less*. If you focus on eating less, you count the number of calories you consume. You keep your calories under a certain limit so that your body can shed excess fat. Now go to your cupboard or your fridge and pull out any food item. On that item, find the caloric value on the label. You will find that all percentages are based on a limit of calories. What does the label base its percentages on? Does it say *"based on 62,000 calories per month"*? No, of course it doesn't. That would seem ridiculous. The label says *"based on 2,000 calories per day."* Are you seeing the significance of this? Is it beginning to come clear to you?

If you were to base your caloric intake on 62,000 calories, that would represent a *monthly* allowance of calories. Keeping track of monthly calorie allowances would be nearly impossible—much too difficult to track. However, the 2,000-calorie limit is based on a *daily* allowance. It is much easier to track your calories on a daily basis. The Dollar Code can be likened to this diet analogy. It is much easier to remember a number that you use *every day*.

Budgeting on a monthly basis simply does not work. It is just too lengthy to manage or remember. This is especially true if we lose control of our spending during the month. If you were to apply the Dollar Code, you would be able to get back on track as soon as the very next day, whereas the monthly budget could put you as much as a month behind.

DOLLAR CODE **TIP #4**

"Learn to think about your spending on a daily basis, rather than at the end of the month. Budgeting on a monthly basis is too overwhelming."

Unlocking Your Code

The Dollar Code will unlock your personal DA (Daily Allowance). This is the amount of money you can spend freely each day. It is the number in your head that you should not exceed for your daily spending. The cool thing about this number is that it will very quickly help you understand how important those "little expenses" are and how fast they can add up.

In its simplest form, the Dollar Code formula is the amount of money you make each month *minus* the amount you are committed to spending each month (on things like your rent or mortgage, car payments, etc.) and then *divided* by the number 31 (which represents the days in the longest months). The amount is always rounded to the nearest dollar. Written out as a formula, it looks like this:

(Money In – Money Out) ÷ 31

Now let's take an example. Let's say that you make $3,000 per month (the amount you receive as take-home pay). And let's say that your monthly recurring and committed expenses (such as your mortgage, car payment, groceries, etc.) come to a total of $2,000. That would leave you with $1,000 of money to spend each month. It initially sounds pretty good, doesn't it? However, once you count going out to dinner a few times, grabbing a few lattes at Starbucks, tickets to the movies, and so on, that $1,000 can disappear pretty quickly. You may not even realize it or remember where it went! *Poof!* But . . . if you apply the Dollar Code to figure out your DA based on the example above, you can calculate the following:

$$(\$3,000 - \$2,000) \div 31 = 32$$

Money In   Money Out

The number 32 is your DA (Daily Allowance), in this example. It represents the *daily amount* of money that can be spent if you expect to keep within your budget. Like the allowance you might have had as a child, this is the amount you now give yourself to spend. It is in real dollars, so the 32 means $32.00.

That means if you spend over $32 in one day, you are *over* your budget limit and you are going further into debt. Are you surprised that $1,000 in spending money each month, broken down to a daily amount, is that low? Let's put it into perspective by using an example of spending.

Hypothetically, you stop by Starbucks in the morning for that latte: $5. You pick up the newspaper: $2. Then you drive to work and park at work for the day: $10. You forgot to pack a lunch, so you grab a sandwich at the sub shop: $8. At 3:00 PM, you need a pick-me-up, so you grab a Snickers bar out of the vending machine: $2. It's not even the end of the workday, and you've already spent a total of $27. Now you have *only $5* left to spend the rest of the day. I hope you don't plan on doing anything that costs more than five bucks, like going to a movie in the evening.

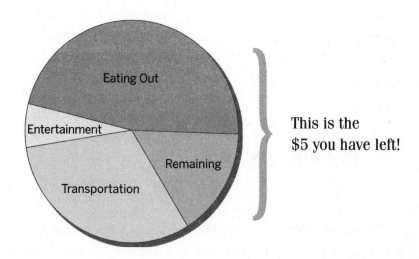

This is the $5 you have left!

Wow . . . are you shocked? This sounds like a typical day, doesn't it? Things sure add up quickly without people even realizing it. It's *scary*, isn't it? Or depressing? Definitely. However, now you have the power to regain control of your spending using the Dollar Code. It will be easier than you think. By making small changes, I *promise* that you will succeed. Of course, your DA may be different from the example used. Follow along and you will be able to figure it out. You don't have to be a mathematician or an accountant, either. It's very easy for anyone.

Let's now take that same day using the Dollar Code system. Seeing how quickly all of the "little" expenses add up, you decide to make that latte at home: $1. You take the train/bus into work: $2. Because your office subscribes to the newspaper, you read that during your break: $0. And you pack a lunch: $4, which includes a snack-size chocolate bar you bought at the convenience store. Now your spending looks like this:

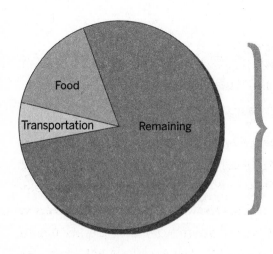

You now have $25 left! You can use this toward a big purchase, a vacation, or savings!

DOLLAR CODE **TIP #5**

"Your Dollar Code is made up of two components: your income and your expenses. Look at your total monthly take-home pay. Then add up all the recurring bills and living expenses that you are committed to. Then divide this by 31."

The Dollar Code system is easy to use and easy to maintain. Unlocking your Code for the first time is a simple, three-step process. I do recommend setting aside some quality, uninterrupted time to complete the initial setup.

STEP ONE:

Gather your **Recurring Bills** and your **Living Expenses**

You will need at least one month's worth of figures from your recurring bills and your living expenses. Ideally, I would suggest using three months of bills to get an accurate average. The reason that three months works better with the Dollar Code is because your expenses can vary month to month. For example, one month your cell phone bill might be $50. The next it might be $40. The trick here is to take the cell phone bill from the *highest* month. Do this with each bill that I have listed below. You want to capture *all* of the bills you are committed to paying each month.

Here's an example of your *recurring bills*:

- ✔ Mortgage payment or monthly rent
- ✔ Insurance on your house
- ✔ Car payment
- ✔ Car insurance
- ✔ Child support
- ✔ Any other expenses that you are *committed* to pay on a recurring basis (bank fees, etc.)—a full listing of these is included in the worksheet at the end of this book

Here's an example of your *living expenses*:

- ✔ Grocery purchases
- ✔ Personal and beauty expenses (such as haircuts, etc.)
- ✔ Gym memberships

For a full list, see the worksheet at the end of this book.

STEP TWO:

Grab your last paycheck stub

For your paychecks (your "Money In"), you want the monthly amount of *take-home* pay you make. Note that you may be paid twice a month, every second week, or once a week. If this is the case, do the conversion to monthly found on the worksheet at the back of the book. Remember to add in any additional checks that are regular, supplemental income that you can count on. If you find this conversion challenging, head to our website (*www .TheDollarCode.com*) and use our free converter. In addition, we're excited to announce that the Dollar Code is now a smartphone app, which works on both iPhones and Android phones and makes doing these calculations and tracking your DA easy! Head over to the Apple or Google Play store on your phone and search for "Dollar Code."

STEP THREE:

Calculate away!

You now apply the formula I gave you in this chapter to calculate your DA! One important thing to remember: If an expense is *not* part of your recurring bills or living expenses, do *not* include it in your calculation. These are "personal expenses" that become part of your daily spending (such as eating out, packs of gum, magazines, movies, etc.). You'll see how to use these in the next section, "Using the Dollar Code."

There is a full worksheet included at the end of the book to assist you in calculating your DA. Again, we've made the Dollar Code calculator available on our website (*www.thedollarcode .com*), or you can use our smartphone app!

Using the Dollar Code

The idea behind the Dollar Code is not about giving up the things you want. It is based on a *daily* allowance. If you go over your daily limit, you must spend less the next day to catch up. The

Dollar Code does not make you give up your morning java or the movies. Rather, it makes you take a step back to assess whether or not you *really* need that thing you are about to buy. Is it something worth sacrificing to stay within your budget, so you won't have to struggle later to come up with the difference that you need to pay a bill or cover an unexpected expense, such as a car repair? Having this awareness and dollar limit in your head is easy to remember. You can even write it down on a little piece of paper or keep track on your smartphone. Doing so, you will likely put a value on each expense and, in turn, cut back on frivolous purchases.

Remember, the idea is to start with the *same amount* each and every day. Your DA is the daily allowance that you have calculated in Step Three above. Each time you make a purchase or spend money that day on any item that you did not use when calculating your DA (i.e., items that are not your recurring or living expenses), you *subtract* that amount from your starting number. For example, if the Dollar Code calculated a DA of **32**, that is the number you start with each day. Say, for example, you buy a pack of gum from the convenience store for $1. You subtract 1 from 32 and you now have **$31** remaining to spend for the day. Later on, you buy a card for your friend's birthday for $5. You then subtract 5 from 31 and you now have **$26** remaining. Your goal is to stay above zero by the end of the day. It's as simple as that!

Will Your DA Ever Change?

The answer is both yes and no. Stay tuned . . . you're going to get a further explanation of this question in the following chapters!

4 Understanding Your Daily Allowance ("DA")

N ow that you have learned how to use the Dollar Code to calculate your DA, you may be shocked and scared at just how low that amount may be. Instead of becoming frantic, you need to put a plan of action into place. Immediately. Pronto. Today.

In this chapter, we will deal with the following situations:

1. The 5-Minute Checkup
   a. Going *over* your DA (i.e., "overspending")
   b. Going *under* your DA (i.e., "carry-over")
2. Increasing your DA
3. Your Quarterly Update

The 5-Minute Checkup

The Dollar Code is, hands-down, the easiest system you could ever use to help you control your finances. Whether you use a pen and paper, a computer, or the smartphone app, it *will* help you stay on course. If you use just a bit of discipline each day, it will help you gain an understanding of your spending so that you can achieve financial freedom. I promise you that.

This bit of discipline I'm talking about is called the "5-Minute Checkup." You do this checkup each and every day, and it takes only five minutes of your time. The best time to do your 5-minute checkup is before you go to bed. Here's how it works and why I want you to do it: Throughout the day, you have likely spent money. With each purchase, you subtract that amount from your DA. At the end of the day, take note of your remaining amount. If it is above zero, give yourself a pat on the back. You have spent within your limit and are on your way to achieving financial freedom. If your number is negative, you have gone over your daily limit. *But* don't beat yourself up because the Dollar Code is all about learning; it's about gaining an understanding of when and how much you spend so that you can control your spending.

Regardless of the amount at the end of the day, there are *two* important reasons for the 5-Minute Checkup:

1. **Evaluation**—take a look at what you spent throughout the day and reflect on *how* you could have decreased this spending. Did you really need all of those items? Remember, this is not about guilt. It is about becoming aware of your spending habits. Perhaps you will look at your daily

spend and think "Yes, I needed that Starbucks latte—it helped get me through my afternoon." If that's the case, don't fret about it. The important thing is that you are consciously thinking about what you are spending. This helps you understand your spending and, again, will help you control it!

2. **Over or Under**—if you have an amount remaining at the end of the day, you have what I call "carry-over." This is like a bonus because you spent less than your daily limit. You now have two choices. You can either add this amount to your next day's dollar amount or you can put this into your Fun Bucket (to save up for a big purchase or a family vacation)—see more about the Fun Bucket later on in this book. Now if you have a negative amount, it means you are over and that you've overspent. In this case, you must *subtract* this amount from tomorrow's daily limit. For example, if your DA is 32, then you must *subtract* it from tomorrow's 32, giving you less that you are able to spend tomorrow!

Increasing Your DA

Once you've used the Dollar Code to figure out your DA, you may be shocked by how low it really is. It doesn't matter how much you make or how great your job is if you live beyond your means. If you're spending more than you are making, you will never get ahead. Your finances will be constantly hanging by a thread, like a cat dangling on a string with just its claws, trying not to fall.

Even if you are surprised to learn how low your DA may be, you must stick with it—no matter what. Previously, I talked about self-discipline and determination to change your spending habits. Now it's time to take it up a notch and work on increasing your DA. Rather than being bummed out about the actual dollar amount you may be looking at, it's now time to stay focused so that you can improve.

⊃ To get your DA higher, you have to either ↑ your Money In or ↓ your Money Out.

The DA you calculate using the Dollar Code may be as low as $10 to $20. It can seem impossible to live on so little per day; yet many people have far less than that in reality. They "live large" and spend frivolously, but in all actuality they may also be using credit cards or living paycheck to paycheck.

Remember, the Dollar Code formula looks at *two* things: *Money In* and *Money Out*. To get your DA higher, you have to either increase your Money In or decrease your Money Out. With a sigh, you may be thinking that is close to impossible, especially if your number is already low and you are used to spending on a whim. However, it can be done. You *can* increase your DA, and I'm going to show you how to do it.

The only way to *increase your Money In* is, really, to make more money. There are many things you can do to make more money, and there are many good books written on how to do it. Because the Dollar Code's purpose and main focus is for you to understand your spending so that you can control it, I won't go into detail on increasing your salary or wages from your job. That is a lesson for another day. However, I do offer tips later on in this book of ways you can earn extra cash.

However, the good news is that there are *many* ways you can *decrease your Money Out,* which, in turn, will increase the daily amount you can spend on personal expenses and still live within your means. All of these ways relate to your recurring bills and living expenses (if you need a refresher on what these are, go back and reread Chapter 3). First of all, when you used the Dollar Code to calculate your DA, you included all of your "must-have" expenses. In doing so, you may have noticed a lot of wasteful items. The things you *need* and are *committed to* are the essentials, such as rent or mortgage payments, insurance, property taxes, groceries, utilities, child support, or a car payment. These must be paid every month in order to live. However, you may find stunning and unexpected wasteful expenses that can be slashed.

Step One is tackling these expenses and evaluating each one to determine if it is a must-have, necessity, or want. Assess each and every bill and truly study it to see if there is any way for you to lower it. Companies are in business to make money, and they count on people to just pay their bills and not look at them. You need to be proactive. Here are some ideas to implement if you want to decrease your Money Out so that you can increase your DA:

- ✔ **Reduce your communications bill.** Many people have a home phone, cell phone, Internet connection, and perhaps multiple phones for each member of their family. Have you thought about why you need all of these things? Do you really talk on the phone that much that you would need both a cell phone and a landline? How much would it save you every month if you gave up one of these things? Let's say you decide you can

live without your home phone and that it costs you $54 every
month. Thinking about it as a yearly expense, that's $648.
However, changing your mind-set to "daily" means adding
nearly $2 to your DA—that's $2 more you'll have every day!
Then if you have extra things on your phones that are unneces-
sary, such as caller ID, call waiting, or bigger calling plans that
you don't even use close to all of the minutes, that's another
dollar or two every single day. You can whittle away these
nickel-and-dime extras one by one. It will take some work to
figure out what those may be the first time. Another way to
reduce your communications bill is to "bundle" your expenses
(these same cell phone, Internet, and perhaps cable expenses).
New plans come out all the time, and a quick phone call to your
communications provider, asking them if they can do anything
to reduce your monthly bills can be extremely worthwhile!

DOLLAR CODE **TIP #6**

**"Start eliminating things that
set you back, things you don't need,
or packages that are too big.
Communications can be a
tremendous money waster for
many families."**

✔ **Call all of your credit card companies.** Ask them to lower your interest rate. If they say; *"No, you don't qualify,"* explain to them that you are thinking about moving your account to another, lower interest-rate card. People often don't realize they have the power to do this. They think they are at the mercy of the high *(gasp!)* 24 to 29 percent interest rates. However, credit card companies have been forced to work with consumers due to the large volume of people who have defaulted or gone through bankruptcy. Credit card companies are far more likely to work with you these days. They may even extend a debt repayment plan, if asked. The point is, you never know unless you ask. So call them all and speak to a manager about getting your interest rate lowered and perhaps eliminating penalties such as over-the-limit or late fees.

✔ **Lower your utility bills.** There are a thousand ways to lower your electric and water bills. Just browse online; there are many sites offering practical and energy-efficient household tips. Type *"Tips to lower my electric bill"* (or water bill) in the search engine browser and you'll get a plethora of ideas.

✔ **Get your grocery bill down.** When you shop, do you pile every type of food in the cart that you think you'll need? Or do you plan? Planning your meals for the week—at least on a list—will help cut expenses greatly. It will avoid impulse buying and adding items that you don't truly need. Junk food typically costs more, so cut down on desserts and chips. You'll see a significant reduction in your grocery bill (and perhaps your waistline)!

✔ **Buy no-name products.** While you're at the grocery store, look for as many *"supermarket house brand"* products as you can. They often have the same quality and ingredients. Some are even made by the same companies that offer the name-brand products. With the average saving being 20 percent or more for each no-name product, you might shave $20 or more off your grocery tab.

✔ **Use what you have in your cupboards.** People, by nature, are hoarders. How many boxes of spaghetti or cans of soup do you already have? People tend to buy new instead of using what they already have in stock. This is just a habit. Use it up before you go grocery shopping next time.

✔ **Get basic cable or none.** How often do you truly watch HBO? Is it often enough to justify the extra $30 to $40 on your cable bill every month (which could work out to a couple of dollars a day)? Oh yeah, it *is* costing you that much, whether you realize it or not. Also, don't forget about the "bundling" idea I shared with you in the tip on communications expenses. And if you have Internet access, you may be able to find shows or movies online for free, or you could subscribe to a service like Netflix that is only a fraction of the monthly cost of cable and allows you to view movies and TV shows as often as you want!

DOLLAR CODE **TIP #7**

"Treat yourself enough but not too often. That way it will mean something."

✔ **Pack a lunch.** Food is something many people falter in when it comes to finances. Breakfast, lunch, and dinner should be made at home. You can bring your lunch instead of eating out or takeout and save as much as $10 or more a day!

✔ **Put off temptations or splurges for a week.** When people make a major purchase, such as a car or a furniture set, they typically sleep on the decision overnight. They rarely say, *"I'll take it!"* upon first sight. So why then do people hastily buy other things? They go to Home Depot and see a cool gadget or new tool and throw it into the cart, or they see a new purse or new shoes and *"have to have it"*! Start developing an "I'll think about it" mentality about *all* purchases, not just the biggies. You may find that an item you wanted in haste is something you will regret later, or you may not even want it as much as you thought at the time. How often will you even wear those four-inch leopard spiked heels, anyway? Why do you honestly need another power drill just because your plug-in drill might have inconvenienced you once? If it gets the job done and is not broken, then keep it.

DOLLAR CODE **TIP #8**

"Think about your impulse buying. It is often the smaller items that will eat you alive. Be conscious of spending habits and decisions."

✔ **Work out at home.** Gym memberships, clothing, and aerobics classes are all expensive. It may be your social outlet, but you can buy everything you need to work out at home (or outside) for about the same amount as two months' gym membership.

✔ **Share a car with your spouse.** Even if it may seem implausible logistically, you'd be surprised at how well this can work and save you in many ways. You or your spouse could carpool with coworkers. The kids could take the bus, couldn't they? You will not only save a lot on the extra car payment, you will save on auto insurance, repairs, vehicle maintenance, and fuel. Everything will be shaved down to one car. As a bonus, it's better for the environment to use less fuel.

✔ **Get a membership to a bulk club.** Supermarkets nickel and dime you on the little things, plus you will find small items that seem tempting. Buying wholesale—such as at Costco, Sam's Club, or BJ's—forces you to evaluate whether or not you need it. You get more for your money: more meat, veggies, snacks, and so forth by buying in larger volume. You can freeze the extras. You'll also avoid putting things into your cart that will put you over your grocery budget (extra sauce, extra snacks, etc., all add up).

✔ **Do laundry only once a week.** Resist the urge to do a batch of laundry for only a few items. Don't run the dryer; just hang up your clothes. You'll save tremendously on both your electric and water bills.

✔ **Pay bills on time.** You may know this and have the best intentions but still always fall into the trap of being a few days late. Those late fees can cost anywhere up to 10 percent of your bill. Do this enough times and all of your bills will be padded. Get caught up! You've heard of paying bills online or automatic bill pay, so use these tools and get with today's times.

✔ **Change insurance companies.** Big insurance companies are vying for your business. Raise your deductible if you can afford to, as this will significantly lower your payment.

Your Quarterly Update

Personal health is a very important thing, and anyone who has battled with their own health knows this all too well. Eating healthy, exercising, and visiting your doctor when you are ill are all important factors in staying healthy. Going for your annual checkup is *also* very important. Like your own personal health, taking care of your financial health is no different!

I recommend doing a financial health checkup quarterly—that is, every three months (or think of it as once every season: spring, summer, fall, and winter). The benefits of doing so are *huge*, and it really takes no time at all. The first step in scheduling your quarterly update is the task of putting it in your calendar. Do me a favor: Put this book down and grab your calendar *now!* Do it before you forget. Record the date that you are going to start doing the Dollar Code. Then flip three months ahead and put in a reminder for your quarterly update. Flip to the next three months ahead and do the same. By scheduling it now, you are committing to keeping your financial health in check!

I am an advocate for scheduling in your quarterly updates. However, there may be times in between these dates that you need to reevaluate or recalculate your Dollar Code. Such circumstances include the following:

✔ Starting a new job

✔ Getting a raise or promotion

✔ Moving (to a new apartment, house, city, etc.)

✔ Buying a new car

✔ Having a baby

✔ Anything else that substantially changes your monthly income or recurring expenses!

DOLLAR CODE **TIP #9**

"Always recalculate your DA as soon as possible if you experience any changes to your income or recurring bills."

Your quarterly update is also a great time to analyze all of your recurring bills and living expenses. Remember to always take the month with the highest bill when using the Dollar Code calculation. Also, your quarterly update is a great time to determine if there are any bills that you have missed when doing your previous calculations. If so, include them!

Recalculating your DA with the Dollar Code is done the same way you did it the first time. Go through the three steps explained previously and you'll arrive at your new number!

5 Credit Cards and the Dollar Code

Credit cards have become a part of our daily lives. As we move to a "cashless society," it will become more and more difficult to avoid using credit cards. I explained in the beginning chapters that credit cards cause us to lose touch with our spending because they separate us from the money we have. They are not a tangible item like cash. It is very easy to *just charge* something without knowing its immediate impact on our finances.

I strongly advocate against the use of traditional credit cards. Even with our society moving to a cashless system, we still have options such as debit cards and prepaid credit cards. The benefit of both of these forms of plastic is that they allow us to use *only* money we already have. A debit card withdraws the money from your bank account the second you use it on a purchase. A prepaid credit card makes you "add" a balance to it via a cash payment or a transfer from your bank account *before* you can use it. Both of these forms of payment are closer to cash, and they are not based on borrowed funds. In addition, they do not charge interest, although they may come with user fees.

We cannot ignore credit cards, however, so I will explain below about the benefits of credit cards, the pitfalls of credit cards, and how they can be incorporated into the Dollar Code system.

Benefits of Credit Cards

There are certain benefits to using the modern credit cards we have available to us. Such benefits can include the accumulation of points that can later be redeemed for travel, gift cards, or even cash back. Many credit cards also offer "insurance"—some offer theft, damage, or loss insurance on purchased items, and others extend their insurance component to the use of rental cars. Each credit card differs in its offerings (including the limitations on the offerings), and I suggest reading the fine print carefully and ensuring you understand what it all means.

Pitfalls of Credit Cards

Again, credit cards separate us from developing a true understanding of cash. It can be extremely easy to charge up items to a credit limit without having the ability to pay back the full amount owed. Many credit cards (especially department store cards) can have extremely high interest rates. Although the monthly payments may not seem large, the high interest rates charged mean you can end up paying much more for an item than its actual cost. It is extremely easy to get into debt by using credit cards, and credit card debt is responsible for many bankruptcies.

Incorporating Credit Cards into the Dollar Code

The great thing about the Dollar Code is that it is a system that gets you back in touch with your spending habits. It is bigger than your understanding of just money, which means that, ultimately, your form of payment for daily items does not matter. Because you are tracking your daily spending and the Dollar Code has calculated an amount that allows you to spend within your means, whether you charge it or pay cash for it is inconsequential. However, if your method of payment is either cash or debit card, your bank account is reduced each time you purchase an item. With a credit card, this does not happen. So . . . how do you account for this? The best way to illustrate is to compare two scenarios:

Scenario One: Using a credit card for all daily expenses

Let's say that Bob uses a credit card for all of his daily expenses. Bob's monthly income is $2,500, and his recurring and living expenses total $1,880 per month. He has used the Dollar Code and calculated his DA (daily spending amount) to be $20 (2,500 less 1,880 and divided by 31). At the start of the month, Bob had $700 in his bank account, and he gets paid on the last day of the month. Assuming that he used up his daily amount each day of the month, his credit card bill at the end of the month would be $620. Bob's scenario would look like this on the last day of the month:

Bob's Bank Account

$700 beginning + $2,500 earned − $1,880 in bills = $1,320

Bob's Credit Card: **$620 owed**

Once Bob pays off his credit card at the end of the month, he has **$700** left in his bank at the end of the month ($1,320 − $620).

Scenario Two: Using cash or debit for all daily expenses

Let's say that Bob uses a debit card for all of his daily expenses. Bob's monthly income is $2,500, and his recurring and living expenses total $1,880 per month. He has used the Dollar Code and calculated his daily amount to be $20 (2,500 less 1,880 and divided by 31). At the start of the month, Bob had $700 in his bank account, and he gets paid on the last day of the month. Assuming that he used up his daily amount each day of the month, his total debit transactions for the end of the month would be $620. Bob's scenario would look like this on the last day of the month:

Bob's Bank Account

$700 beginning + $2,500 earned − $1,880 in bills − $620 in debit card transactions = $700

At the end of the month, Bob has **$700** in his bank account.

Under either scenario, Bob ends up with the same amount in his bank account. Therefore, it does not matter which method of payment is used. The key is that the credit card statement must be *paid off* at the end of the month. When you first begin using the Dollar Code, you may owe a credit card balance. The goal is to use any remaining funds in your bank account at the end of the month to pay down your credit card as quickly as possible. I will provide tips later on in the book to help you with this!

6 Tips to Increase Your Cash and Decrease Your Daily Expenses

Increase Your Cash

Take a look around your house. Do you have clutter? Can you see any items you no longer use? Getting rid of items you no longer use or want can be a very valuable source of cash! Sell items you're not using instead of keeping them in the closet. With such great inventions like eBay, Kijiji, and Craigslist, it has become incredibly easy to sell used items. People will buy anything! Jeans, kid's stuff, antiques, and even the strangest things you have stashed away are just sitting there, waiting to make you money. Start with listing just an item or two. Soon you will see the demand out there for your used items.

Once you sell an item, you will have increased your cash. Now, what do you do with that cash? Well, it's completely up to you. Because you already have your DA (calculated using the Dollar Code), you are free to do whatever you want with that cash. Perhaps you want to save it for a larger purchase or a family vacation (see the Fun Bucket idea later on in this book), or maybe you want to pay down a few bills or get your bank account out of overdraft. You can also add it to your savings. It's *your* choice!

Decrease Your Daily Expenses

For starters, you will have to resist the urge to splurge. People waste money on countless things every day: things they don't even realize. As I explained previously, it's okay to buy that coffee in the morning. If it makes you happy, and you are comfortable with the expense decreasing your DA, then go for it. I'm not here to tell you what you can and can't have. However, what I can't stress to you enough is that your attitude about the money you currently spend must change.

Resist the temptation to spend money on things like the following:

- ✔ Eating out excessively (like every day) and take-out
- ✔ Buying things often for friends (a pack of smokes, candy bars, snacks, etc.)
- ✔ More than one coffee or "happy purchase" per day

✔ Frequent entertainment that costs money (try 1
   things to do, like going to the beach, etc.)

✔ Splurges when shopping. When you shop for clc
   example, go with a preset budget and do not fall prey to the
   "buy two, get one free" ploy unless it is part of your overall
   DA amount

✔ Impulse buys on TV infomercials or through tricky salespeople

✔ Things you just don't really need

As part of this exercise in self-discipline, you need to assess what you can and can't live without. Temptation is all around you, but you must be motivated to change your mentality about money. Can you live comfortably without that extra pair of shoes that caught your eye? Do you absolutely *have* to have a pair of jeans that cost $90, or can you find discounted stores that may have designer names for $40? Go to the discounted stores first when shopping and avoid the mall!

DOLLAR CODE **TIP #10**

"To avoid impulse buying, put your purchase off for a day. If you've forgotten about it or it seems less important, you didn't really need it in the first place."

Many material possessions are a big waste of money. So is going out frequently. We all love to have fun, myself included. However, it is financially irresponsible to spend (waste) money on going out all the time. Try to think of other ways to have a good time, rather than eating or drinking away your whole paycheck. If you do eat out, do you really have to order appetizers and the most expensive meal there is? Can you drink soda or water instead of expensive liquored drinks? It may be part of the fun in going out to eat, but do this too often and your budget will be devoured right before your very eyes.

No one is here to judge you. What you do with your money is totally up to you. I am simply here to point out and give you that nudge of encouragement to begin living within your means. You will always have the proverbial angel sitting on one shoulder and the devil sitting on the other.

The angel says, *"Save your money for vacation this summer."*

The devil says, *"Just buy it now, what's the harm?"*

Who will *you* listen to?

7 Savings, Emergency Funds, and the Fun Bucket

Saving for the Future

To plan for the future and get ahead financially, we're told we need to save money. However, doing just that can be easier said than done. Like anything else that relates to your finances, saving money takes discipline and a plan. The best recommendation I can give for you to incorporate your savings plan into the Dollar Code is to include it as one of the items when calculating your DA. Even if the amount you are able to include is small in comparison to your other expenses, it's a start. I always tell clients that the most important thing is the start. Begin by including between 1 and 10 percent of your monthly take-home pay in your Dollar Code calculation. For example, if you make $2,000 in take-home pay a month, add between $20 (which is 1 percent) or $200 (which is 10 percent) into your Dollar Code calculation.

An excellent method of enforcing this savings pattern is to have a set amount automatically withdrawn from your bank account each month and placed into a savings account. Ensure that this bank account does not link with your debit card—this way, you are not able to withdraw funds on a whim or impulse. I will explain more about savings accounts in the 20 Percent Rule, which I talk about later in this chapter.

Setting up a savings account will also make you feel empowered. You will realize that you can be in control of your money instead of letting your money be in control of you—and that you can, in fact, save some of it for those unexpected dilemmas. What a great feeling!

Set Up an Emergency Fund

An unexpected car repair, a job loss, a catastrophe with the kids, or a trip to the vet could really set you back financially if you have to use money that you were going to pay bills with. With an emergency fund, you have a buffer you can use without affecting your monthly bill payments. Just think of how much less stress you will feel if you have an unexpected expense come up and you don't have to scramble to find the funds for it—because you already have the money set aside. How freeing is that!

DOLLAR CODE **TIP #11**

"**Make it inconvenient to have access to your own savings account. Having to withdraw it at the bank will deter you from impulsively taking it out to use on spontaneous items.**"

Financial gurus tell us we need to set aside three to six months of basic living expenses as an emergency fund. Now, how do you do this using the Dollar Code? Initially, you will have to make the emergency stash one of the required figures in your Dollar Code calculation. Similar to your savings plan, I recommend beginning by including between 1 and 10 percent of your net take-home pay, the same as with your savings plan, in your Dollar Code calculation.

The 20 Percent Rule

By incorporating both savings and emergency fund compo-nents into your Dollar Code calculation, you will notice a side effect: your bank balance will grow. How exciting is this! (Now, if this is *not* happening, then you must figure out why. Perhaps your recurring bills or living expenses are more than you had thought when you initially used the Dollar Code to calculate your DA. If this is the case, go immediately to the quarterly update section in this book and recalculate! However, the side effect of your bank account balance *growing* is most likely happening.) This is the point at which you have to *avoid temptation to spend that extra money* and apply what I call the *20 Percent Rule*. So what is this rule all about?

The 20 Percent Rule is your way of easily converting the growing dollars in your bank account into your savings and emergency funds. When your bank account hits 20 percent of your take-home pay, you must take that amount of money out and put it somewhere else. For example, if you make $2,000 in take-home pay a month, you take action when your bank balance reaches an extra $400 (2000 x 20%). As I stated above, you need to put that somewhere else. My best recommendation is to open up *two* high-interest savings accounts (yes, two). This is where it is important to talk to your banker. As a side note, a *very* important thing is developing a good relationship with your banker. This is a great way to start doing this!

Tell your banker that you want to put your extra money aside into two separate accounts: one for savings and one for an emergency fund. What you're going to do is take that 20 percent that you withdrew from your regular bank account and split it *equally* between the two accounts. Half of it will go into savings and half of it will go into your emergency fund. Ensure that neither of these accounts are linked to your debit card—this stops you from making impulse decisions on spending these amounts. You must physically go into the bank or log on to your online banking to use these funds.

Your banker will likely offer you a few good suggestions in setting up the accounts. My recommendation is to include the savings amount as part of your 401k plan (called the RRSP in Canada). The emergency fund portion could be placed in a *high-interest* savings account. Remember, it is important to talk to your banker and have these accounts set up properly. While you're at it, ask for additional financial advice—after all, you're getting this advice from a trained professional for free!

The absolute coolest thing about the 20 Percent Rule is watching your money grow. When it is growing in your regular bank account, you can almost make it a game to get that amount up to 20 percent as quickly as possible. It can actually become a form of entertainment! Then, after you've set up your savings and emergency fund accounts, you can watch those amounts grow, and you will be *making* interest on your money instead of *paying* interest. Take *pride* in all of this—you are saving for your future (and perhaps your family's future), *and* you are also relieving yourself of the stress of unexpected expenses!

The Fun Bucket

A Fun Bucket is different from a savings account. This is something that you will keep in your home to hide a "private stash" of money—something that you can access on the weekends or periodically for treats. Your Fun Bucket can be anything—it can be a safe, water bottle, box, a pail, a piggy bank, ... anything! If you have children, I encourage your whole family to get involved in the Fun Bucket. Decorate it. Highlight it. Make it something that you want to put cash and coins into for fun family outings or trips.

The Fun Bucket is a place that you will throw extra money into from time to time, perhaps when you have days that you didn't spend all of your daily amount. If your DA is 30 and you've only spent $18 on any given day, then you can put the remaining $12 in your Fun Bucket. This is extra money that you can take out for "fun stuff" and splurges that you *don't have to feel guilty about in the least!* After all, the money was extra that you had to spend, but as you become better and better about saving, you may find more enjoyment in having more of it around for fun stuff. Treat yourself to the movies, the zoo, a night out, or anything you want. You can use it in lieu of your daily amount, and spend it however you wish.

The Fun Bucket technique is different from your savings account, and you will save for it differently. The savings account and emergency fund should be part of your Dollar Code calculation (even if it is only a small amount to start out with), whereas the Fun Bucket is money left over that you didn't spend on days that your daily amount was not used to its full capacity.

8 The Dollar Code Recap and Frequently Asked Questions (FAQs)

S ome people don't budget very well for two reasons. One is time. They think that budgeting is too time-consuming, and in today's fast-paced society it is simply not a priority. We live in a world where we fly from one appointment to another, with busy families, work obligations, extracurricular activities, and social events that leave budgeting on the back burner. Most people think nothing of spending $3 here and $5 there on frivolous things that are often impulse purchases. And many more people think that budgeting equates to being a "tightwad," in other words, a person who is so frugal and caught up in saving that he or she does not allow any extra for fun. This is simply not true!

The second reason that people fail with budgeting is because they lack the know-how. Unfortunately, with all of the great academic programs we learn in school, managing finances is not on the agenda. Of course, some people may have to take accounting in college; however, this is not a requirement, and even accounting classes do not truly delve into the matters of personal budgeting. Therefore, it is up to parents to teach their children how to budget. Yet many parents of today are not so good at managing finances themselves and do not provide the best role models to their children when it comes to living within their means.

One of my goals and purpose for writing this book is to change that. By offering such a *simple* method of calculating a daily amount (your DA), the Dollar Code fits in easily with the fast-paced lifestyle of today's society. People live in the moment and often do not think about the consequences of their spending. They somehow think they can "make it up" later if they overspend, and then get caught in a trap at the end of the month when a certain bill comes due and they are suddenly short on cash.

Let's go over your Dollar Code calculation one more time just to give you a recap and to make sure it is thoroughly engrained in your mind. The object here is to take *all of your necessary bills* and make a list of the totals.

Remember. . . it's as easy as 1—2—3:

1. Make a list of *all* of your monthly bills, going back at least *three* months to figure out an accurate tally of your monthly expenses. Some of your bills may change from month to month, so go by the highest month. Use this amount whenever a bill fluctuates. Grab every single necessary bill, including your mortgage or rent, insurance, vehicle payment, child care expenses, phone, utilities, groceries, and any other fees that are *must-pay expenses*.

2. Gather your last paycheck stub as well as any other extra income earned, as long as it is money you can count on and not one-time earnings.

3. Subtract your monthly expense total from your net income. For example, if your monthly income is $5,000 and your expenses are $3,800, then you will be left with a total of $1,200. That sounds good, right? Next, divide the $1,200 by 31. This is the number of days in a month. Although some months have only thirty or twenty-eight days, you should use 31 as your dividing calculation because it will give you the most conservative DA.

What is your DA? Using the example above, mine is $38 (rounding to the nearest low dollar). That means I am allowed to spend $38 every day without going over my budget. Wasn't that easy? As you can see, you don't even have to be a rocket scientist to figure out your DA! All you need is common sense and perhaps ten minutes of time. This should put your mind at ease that learning the Dollar Code is not difficult, intimidating, or complicated in any way.

Don't forget, if you have extra money that you did not spend out of your DA at the end of each day, you can throw it into your Fun Bucket!

Dollar Code Frequently Asked Questions

Okay, so now that you know how to use the Dollar Code to calculate your DA, let's dig a little deeper and give you further explanation as to how it works. Remember, the concept with the Dollar Code is to keep it *simple*. Your Dollar Code is made up of only two components (your monthly income and your monthly spending). It is calculated by subtracting all of your committed monthly expenses from your monthly income and then dividing that number by 31.

Even though neither one of us may be rocket scientists, you may still have questions about how it works and about how you can best manage to stick to it.

- ♦ **Every month does not have thirty-one days. Why do we divide by 31?**
  - In order to keep it simple, we use the higher number in your Dollar Code calculation to make sure that you don't end up with extra days at the end of the month. For example, February has only twenty-eight days, and four other months have thirty. Because the majority of the months in our yearly calendar have thirty-one days, it is best to use the higher number so as not to fall back on your actual daily spending amount.
  - This is the same principle that is applied when using the "most expensive month" when calculating your expenses.

I recommend tallying the past three months of bills and using the month with the *highest* bill, rather than just using one month to gauge. This will eliminate seasonal fluctuations and discrepancies where some bills may greatly differ.

♦ **What if I get paid weekly or every second week?**

- Convert your earnings to a "daily" amount and then multiply that figure by 31 to come up with the Money In portion of your Dollar Code calculation. For example, if you get paid every week, take your net pay (the amount you take home), and divide it by the number of days in a week (7) and then multiply it by 31. If you get paid every other week, divide that number by 14 and then multiply by 31. If you get paid twice a month, take that number and multiply it by two. It's that simple!

♦ **What if I'm paid by commission or if my monthly pay fluctuates?**

- You may be in a situation where you don't have a steady paycheck. Perhaps you are in a sales job or self-employed. In this situation, look at your pay for the past three months and take the month with the *lowest* amount. If this is too difficult, take the total amount of pay that you've received in the past three months and divide by three (it's like taking an average).

♦ **How often should I use the Dollar Code to recalculate my DA?**

- I recommend recalculating it every three months (quarterly). To keep it easy, you could think of each quarter as a "season"—recalculate each spring, summer, fall, and winter! A lot can change in three months. Hypothetically, you could get a raise, utilities could go up, or you could apply some of the savings tips I've given you within this book to reduce your monthly bills. Any number of things could take place in relation to your income. That is why it is so important to do a reassessment of your income at least once every season or as things occur that can affect the DA you have been using. As a further tip, mark every three months in your calendar as a reminder to recalculate your DA. Do it *now* so that you don't forget!

DOLLAR CODE **TIP #12**

"When looking at your three-month period, use the lowest amount of pay and the highest bill amounts."

- Once you calculate your DA, from that point on keep your monthly bills in a "special place" for the next three months. Then use the same principle I have explained to you when recalculating. Enter the month with the highest bill for each category to determine the most up-to-date DA to use. Imagine how excited you will be when you notice that after a quarterly checkup, your DA may have increased!

DAILY USE

♦ **What do I do if I have money left over at the end of the day?**
  - Well, for starters, that's *awesome*! If your DA is 38 and you have $8 left when the day is over, that means you've been

really smart and disciplined with your spending. It should feel good, knowing that you are sticking to your budget and even making progress. Now there are two options you have:

1. You get to treat yourself (see how *fun* this can be?). Remember the Fun Bucket? You can add the extra $8 to your secret stash and use it to splurge on anything you choose

2. . . . you can add the extra $8 to your DA for the next day. This is a perfect idea for those times when you want to buy items that are more costly than your DA permits. I will explain this a bit further as you keep reading.

♦ What do I do if I go "over" my limit?

- First of all, I encourage you *not* to do that. Spending more than your DA defeats the whole purpose of sticking to a budget and, just like sticking to a diet, this is a big no-no. It's like eating a big piece of cheesecake when you are trying to lose weight. The Dollar Code is a concept of gaining control of your finances. Nevertheless, we are all human. No one is perfect. Therefore, if you do go over on your DA, you *must* take it off the next day's amount—or even two or three days if the overage is really bad. No excuses, ifs, ands, or buts! I'm serious!

♦ How do I buy items that are more than my DA?

- Ah, this is a very good question. This concept is all about *planning* and is another reason why the Dollar Code is so important as it relates to budgeting. If you want to buy an extra pair of shoes, a new golf club, a new outfit, or just need money for any reason that may come up, it may cost more than your DA allows you to spend. Now, you will have three choices:

1. As I've explained above, the first way to buy something that is more than your DA is to spend less on other days until you have accumulated the amount you need. For example, if your DA is 30 and you are only allowed to spend $30 every day without busting your budget, but the new golf club is $100, you will need to spend less than $30 each day until you reach the extra funds that are needed to buy the club. Every day your DA will continue to increase. Continuing with the example, you could spend $20 a day for seven days and that should give you enough to buy the golf club. The best part is that now you can buy your new golf club guilt-free!

2. The *second* way to buy items that will go over your DA is to set aside the extra money you have each day from your DA and put it into your Fun Bucket. This way you can max out your daily spending amount every day but continue to have cash accumulating toward the item you really want. Very often a funny thing happens, though. Some people, after faithfully adding to their stash every day, will then realize that the item they longed for is no longer something they want, even after they have accumulated enough money. This method helps to avoid impulse spending.

3. A third option is to bring only enough each day that you will be allowed to spend. In other words, you can cut your own allowance. So instead of thinking that your daily spending amount for the day will be $30, you can bring only $20. If you don't have it with you, then you won't be able to spend it!

♦ **How do I plan for other things—like a vacation I want to take, gifts I want to buy for others, amounts I want to donate to charity, or things like that?**

- Simple! You can *include* these items in your Dollar Code calculation. There are two ways to achieve this:

  1. Let's say you want to take a holiday or vacation that you think will cost $600, and you know that it will be two months from now. Simply divide the amount by the number of days. In this example you would take $600 and divide it by 60 and then reduce that number from your DA for the next sixty days. In case you don't have a calculator, that equals $10 per day. If your DA is normally 30, then for the next sixty days you will make it 20. I would suggest putting that $10 per day into your Fun Bucket or somewhere safe. But imagine how much fun it will be to count that wad of cash as you leave for vacation, especially knowing that your trip is paid for and that you will not have to worry about debt or repayment.

  2. You can also factor the vacation into your daily spending amount in the initial spreadsheet that you use to figure out your daily number. By adding it as an expense, you will be able to automatically build it into your DA without feeling guilty about breaking your budget.

- For planned charity giving or things that are of a regular nature (constant, or recurring), just add in the expected monthly giving amount when calculating your DA!

♦ **Does it matter if I'm paying cash, credit card, or other when doing the Dollar Code system?**

- This is a very good question. It doesn't matter how you apply the Dollar Code or with what method of payment.

Let me explain. Because of the Dollar Code concept, if you are not spending more than you make, then it really doesn't matter *how* you spend it. If you work the Dollar Code system properly and stick to it exactly the way it has been explained, there will always be enough money to pay off your credit card when your statements come in the mail. That is because you have *planned* for it. It's automatically included in your DA!

DOLLAR CODE **TIP #13**

"Although it doesn't matter which method of payment you use to apply to your DA, cash should always be your top choice."

Now, let me add a disclaimer: I am in no way an advocate of using credit cards. The best method of payment for anything you want or need is still cash. Cash is king. Cash is real. By using cash you will get a true sense of something that is leaving your possession to obtain something you want or need, and that is very important. Using credit cards often defeats the purpose of conquering your debt and is less tangible than cash. It is borrowed money, and many people use them with the attitude that they can be paid later. However, some credit cards do have benefits. Some offer travel points and others offer air miles or sky miles. Plus everyone needs a credit card to rent a car or sometimes to make a purchase online. My advice is to use your best judgment. As long as you can remain disciplined with your daily spending amount, credit cards are not always evil.

Tactics for Learning the Dollar Code

Learning the Dollar Code may seem life transforming at first. It may seem like an epiphany. The very realization of managing your budget and not living paycheck to paycheck will become empowering. You will feel liberated and more in control of your money, which may flow into other areas of your life. By not constantly stressing over money and wondering how you will make it from one week to the next, you may feel a sense of *freedom*. That's right: *Freedom!* It takes a bit of time to "get it" and to totally grasp it, seize it, and take the reins, but once you do, you will be much happier.

Once you start using and applying the Dollar Code, you will notice many other positive changes in your life. Your attitude will change and you may develop a new sense of confidence in yourself. Rather than money having control over you and having to avoid bill collectors for late payments, you will be empowered to pay your bills on time and to know that you can afford the few splurges that you choose to spend your money on. Money is just a piece of paper, yet most people become a prisoner to its power.

Here are a few pointers for you to embrace the Dollar Code concept and to properly apply it for ultimate success:

✔ Figure out your DA with the Dollar Code calculation. Then at the beginning of the week or when you get paid, take out and

set aside *each day's* total that you are allowed to spend. Get a
calendar that separates by day and set the allotted amount in a
small envelope for each day, or use some similar method.
Resist the urge to tap into the cash for future days.

✔ Stop thinking about next week, next month, and next year.
Think about *today* and making it through the day. Remain
focused on your goal of sticking to your DA today instead of
worrying about the future.

✔ If you lack the willpower or discipline to control the temptation
to tap into money that you have set aside for tomorrow's daily
spending amount (or the next day, and so on), then make a
routine that works for you. For example, you could write
yourself a daily check for the amount of your DA and cash it
every morning on your way to work. Writing a check prevents
you from taking out too much money from an ATM or from
tapping into cash that you have on hand.

✔ Imagine that your DA is all the money you have in the world.
This may prevent you from frivolous spending if you know that
you must safeguard the cash at hand and use it wisely.

✔ Be conscious of your daily spending amount before relinquish-
ing any money for anything. Whether it is for a can of soda or
a candy bar at the vending machine at work, or a dollar spent
at a toll booth, or a 99-cent hamburger at a fast-food joint, all
of these frivolities will count toward your DA. So don't forget
about the seemingly petty things because they count, too!

✔ Make the Dollar Code fun by giving yourself challenges.
For example, if your DA is 35 you could say, "Today I will try to
come home with an extra $5." By challenging yourself you may
be more likely to save rather than spend that money on something meaningless, *and* you will feel a sense of accomplishment.

✔ Treat yourself whenever you have reached milestones. You can even plan your treats at the beginning of the week. For example, on Monday you could tell yourself that if you accomplish your goal of saving an extra $5 every day from your DA, you will go to the beach. However, if you fail and go over your DA, you will have to compensate by working an extra two hours of overtime.

There are a number of ways you can make using and applying the Dollar Code to your life fun, and you may think of other ideas, as well. The whole point of this is to really begin applying that daily number to your life. Stick your DA number on your mirror or repeat it to yourself every morning ten times. Do whatever works best for you. The main message here is that you must embrace the Dollar Code and not just use it for a couple of weeks and then go back to your old ways. This is a new "lifestyle budget" that you can use for life!

Forming New Habits
to Stay on Track

As you may be all too aware, people tend to develop bad habits in many aspects of their lives. You could say that skipping breakfast is a bad habit but that perhaps it does not suffer the same consequences as having a bad habit of spending your whole paycheck every Friday after you get paid.

Part of becoming fiscally responsible means adopting new habits that are better for you. The first step is to develop an awareness of your finances. Here are some ideas on adopting better budgetary habits:

1. Set aside one day every month—either the first Sunday or the last—to sit down for a couple of hours and look over what you have for bills. Get out a calendar and record the days when certain bills are due. After the bill is paid, cross it off the list or use a highlighter to indicate that it is paid.

2. At the same time as your monthly review and Dollar Code evaluation, check to make sure that your DA is not off balance. Especially in the beginning, you may need to make adjustments in case you forgot to include anything. Make a short list of questions and check them off, one by one. You can include things like the following:

   ✔ Have I been faithfully applying my DA every day without cheating?

   ✔ Are there any bills that I forgot to include in my initial list of expenses?

   ✔ Am I able to pay my bills on time, and if not, what can I do to make adjustments?

   ✔ Is there any money left over that I can save?

   ✔ Do I feel like the Dollar Code is making a difference in my monthly budget?

   ✔ Have I had to sacrifice anything that I feel is very important to my well-being or routine?

   ✔ Am I on the right track?

   ✔ Is my lifestyle not in line with my Dollar Code?

   These are just a few questions you can use to make assessments and help you remain focused on your goal of getting out of debt or freeing up more cash flow. You can make your own list and add to it as needed.

3. Another good habit is to continue striving toward new goals. Without goals you will just be going through the motions like a robot, and you will probably fail. Goals help you stay on track. Write down where you want to be in three months, six months, or even a year from now. This will help you to see clearly and to stick to your plan.

Making Your DA a Habit

As you become better and better at sticking to your DA, it will become a habit that you cannot live without. You will be able to keep track of your daily spending amount in your head and, over time, you will notice that your finances will begin to change.

DOLLAR CODE **TIP #14**

"In order to keep track of your DA in your head, simply deduct every purchase as you go about your day."

Forming the Dollar Code as a habit is a matter of just simple math at a very fundamental level. In the morning your daily spending amount will begin with the DA, which will remain the same each day until your income increases or your expenses decrease. You can do this in your head every time you shop or spend. So let's use 40 as your DA.

In the morning you go and get a coffee; deduct $3. You buy gas on the way to work: $10. Now you are down to $27. Instead of bringing lunch, a few coworkers ask you to go grab a sub. Deduct $6. Now you have $21 and the day is only half over. By mid-afternoon you are ready for an energy drink, so you buy one out of the vending machine at work. That's another $2. Before you know it, you have "nickeled and dimed" yourself all day!

⊃ **The DA (your spending amount) is your discretionary (or disposable) income, not the same income you are using to pay your bills. It is important to know this!**

Using your DA will make you less likely to do this, knowing you will affect your primary number and that you may not have enough by the end of the day to do the things you need.

Important: Anytime you spend money and there is change involved ("cents"), round the DA to the highest number.

DOLLAR CODE **TIP #15**

"Whenever there is change involved in your purchase, round it up to the higher number. So $6.39 becomes $7. This is another method to keep you from going over."

Ten Tips to Easily Decrease Spending

Use these strategies to increase your financial health by decreasing your expenses:

1. Never pay *just* the minimum amount due on a credit card. Always pay more than what is requested. You will be surprised at how much quicker you can pay your credit cards off—and you will save a *lot* of money on interest payments!
2. Skip just one "luxury" a month that you would normally splurge on!
3. Pay off credit cards or loans with small balances first. Those annoying $500-limit cards can make your debt seem daunting, especially since they all have different due dates. Having too many credit cards can become a ball and chain that binds you and leaves you strapped. Get rid of 'em! Cut 'em up!
4. Take on the "pay with cash" mentality. Ask yourself: *"If I can't afford it now, will I be able to afford it later? Better yet, will I want to pay for it later?"*
5. Call all of your creditors (credit card companies, etc.). This will be an afternoon well spent. Many people don't realize they can negotiate. Ask them what "they" can do to help you. By lowering your interest rate, you will have a better likelihood of repayment. They know this! If some say no initially, ask for a manager, as managers can usually do more for you than the normal customer service representatives.

6. If you have a savings account, use most of it toward debt. This idea scares people but is worth it in order to get out of your situation. Just leave enough in case of an emergency, such as your car breaking down or for a situation in which your paycheck does not arrive on time, and so on. Then use the rest to pay down debt. You can rebuild your savings later when your income and your DA goes up.

7. If you have a lot of debt but still have good credit, consider negotiating with one of your credit card vendors to get a low-interest transfer of other debts. Let's say you have six credit cards, but many of them are high-interest department store credit cards. It's smarter to put all of those on one low-interest card then cut up the rest of the cards and close the accounts. It's a lot easier to manage *one* payment than six, and this also helps you tackle the debt faster.

8. Make small sacrifices. At one time you may have thought that buying a generic brand instead of a designer brand was preposterous. In most cases, there really is no noticeable difference. What about going to the fancy spa for a haircut? Instead, opt for the barbershop or regular hair salon!

9. Make a weekly plan for your meals. Pick a day each week that you sit down and write out each meal you will have for the next seven days. From that, make your grocery list before you head out to the store. Include this in your family time, preparing what you can ahead of time with your kids, and freezing the meals for easy heating and serving later on.

10. Put off making a purchase by one week. Who knows, when next week comes, you may not want or need that item any longer!

Having a Savings Account and Emergency Fund

For many people, having a savings or emergency fund seems like a faraway dream. That is because they live every day in survival mode. When money is tight, it causes a whole string of events. You're always flying by the seat of your pants, just hoping the utilities will not get shut off or hoping that you will have enough money to fill up the gas tank to get to work. Some people live in this mode so long they see no other way. Savings account? Why, that's only for the rich folks, right?

Wrong! *You* need an emergency fund, no matter who you are. Everyone needs to plan for the unexpected because there will always be something that comes up at the last minute. What if suddenly you need a new alternator or clutch in your car? What if suddenly you need a root canal and don't have dental benefits covered under your health insurance? What if suddenly your beloved dog gets sick and needs to go to the vet? The "what ifs" are reasons you need an emergency fund.

However, having the contingency money for those "just in case" occurrences can save you—*big time.* Consider your emergency fund as the life preserver of your finances as you sail through life. If you get thrown overboard, you wouldn't want to be without it.

How much should you save, and how can you do it if you happen to be living on the month-to-month plan? Well, using your

DA will certainly help you to build that savings account and emergency fund. Here are some strategies for you to build up a stash of cash without going over your daily spending amount and without getting in a bind:

- ✔ Apply the 20 Percent Rule and open up a savings account and an emergency fund account. Don't get a debit card associated with your savings account—make it as inconvenient as possible to withdraw from your savings account. You could also open it in another town at a credit union that has only one branch. That way every time you may be tempted to borrow, it will take you a while to get there, and you may not go simply because of the inconvenience.

- ✔ See if your company offers an automatic payroll deduction opportunity with your paycheck. You could allocate as little as $10 each week to be automatically withdrawn and placed in the savings account you opened. This will be an amount you will never notice, and it will therefore be easier to save.

- ✔ If you do not have the option of automatic withdrawals, just pretend your savings account is a bill. You could pay it biweekly or once a month, much the same as you would pay your cable or water bill.

- ✔ Quit bad habits, such as smoking! Not only is it bad for your health, but, with the high cost of this terrible habit, it is one of the biggest money-wasters of all time. Let's say you spend $5 to 6 every day on cigarettes. If you quit, keep stashing that $5 to 6 dollars a day away into your savings. You'll be amazed at how much better you will feel both health-wise and financially just by eliminating this one nasty habit. Contact your doctor or a local association for help if you need it; these are readily available, and they are willing to help you!

✔ After you pay off a debt you owe, such as your car payment, a credit card, or personal loan, continue making the payments to yourself instead of the bank. Just send the money to your savings account instead!

✔ Overbudget for groceries or necessities. What this means is that after you review your monthly or biweekly grocery tab, pad the amount in your Dollar Code calculation. Let's say you spend $200 every two weeks on groceries. Add an extra $25 or so to that amount and put the money in your savings every time you go grocery shopping. Better yet, if you happen to spend *less than* what you anticipated, add that number in to your contingency fund as well. If you spend $175 on groceries, then in theory you have budgeted for $225 and that leaves you $50 to put in your safety stash.

✔ Don't add any bonuses into your income. If your boss gives you a holiday bonus, or if you get paid for unused sick days, and so forth, treat that money as "unexpected" income. Use what I call the "third" mentality: divide that received money into three— put the first amount into savings, use the second amount to pay down debt, and put the third amount into your Fun Bucket!

✔ Anytime you do extra work on the side that is beyond your anticipated paycheck, again, use the "third" mentality and allocate it to savings, debt, and your Fun Bucket!

✔ Sell some things you don't want. Have a yard sale or sell individual used things on eBay that you no longer use or need. As they say, "One man's trash is another's treasure." After you do sell it, just put the money in your savings account instead of spending it on more junk you don't need.

✔ Some people have success by opening a Christmas Savings Club. This can be very successful because you won't even miss the money, and you have a choice when you set up the account for it to be $5, $10, $20, or any amount of your choice that is deducted weekly.

✔ A few experts recommend tipping yourself in addition to tipping waitstaff whenever you go out. For example if you leave your server $6 for a meal, then set aside the same amount for your savings account.

✔ Cut back on something you don't need and use that money toward your savings account. How many times have we all gone to the store to get one or two items and then end up leaving with three or four bags full of more things? Whenever you pick something up to buy, ask yourself if this is a "need" or "want." If you can live without it, set it down and walk away. Better yet, run!

How much should you have in your emergency fund? Most experts (including me) will tell you that three months' income is best. However, if you can do more, then just keep going with it. You need to have a goal in the beginning so that you have a tangible amount to strive for. Start with a goal of $1,000 and build it into three months' income. Whether you have $25 or $2,500, the important thing is to *start now* and build your emergency fund.

9 Become Part of the Dollar Code Revolution

As I explained in the Introduction, the Dollar Code is more than a book. It is a *concept*. What I really mean is that a book is something you read for pure enjoyment or to obtain information or knowledge about something. While that is partially the goal of my book, it goes much deeper than just sharing mere knowledge.

A concept, on the other hand, is a plan, intention, or an idea. The Dollar Code is a concept that is intended to transform one's financial situation. It is not really just a book that you pick up and read and then put on the bookshelf. The goal is to have you *apply* the principles I am sharing, and then carry the "magic number" (your DA) with you every day as you go about your day-to-day routine. You should develop a consciousness and inner knowing of exactly where you are, yet in the simplest of ways. All you have to remember is *one number*. That's it! As brilliantly simple as it sounds, things do happen and some people embrace the concept and run with it, while others simply read about it and then just put it on the back burner. I am helping you discover the one number (i.e., your daily spending amount) that will change your life. In the end, though, it is up to you. It is *your* choice to use and apply this number to your daily life!

I read a quote written by Richard Eskow, who is a senior fellow with The Campaign for America's Future, on the organization's website. Paraphrasing song lyrics originally written by John Lennon about God, he said: "*Money is a concept by which we measure our pain.*" That attitude defines the mind-set of today's society. The economy within the past decade has been an eye-opening experience not just within North America but on a global level. People's attitude toward money is that how much (or how little) they have defines them as a person. Many people feel envious of someone who has a lot of money, and they wish they could be in the other person's shoes. On the other hand, when we come across someone who is homeless, we may feel pity or grateful for what little money we do have. It could always be better, but it could always be worse. Being happy with where you are in your relationship with money is just as essential as your relationships with humans.

When I originally conceived the Dollar Code, my goal was that it would help individuals. Since I had already experienced the positive effects of the Dollar Code in my own life, I saw the huge potential for it to catch on and become an easy "secret" that could be spread to everyone. We can all read about the Dollar Code. We can all put the Dollar Code into action for our own situations. But what I want most of all is for everyone to share the Dollar Code. By sharing the Dollar Code, we do two things:

1. We develop a deeper understanding of managing our money by using the Dollar Code; and
2. We develop a *support* system.

Developing a Deeper Understanding of the Dollar Code

When you share, you engage others. You not only become the student, but you also become the teacher. School may not do a good job in teaching people about money, but it does teach students how to learn.

How many classes have you been in where you have had to do a presentation? I remember from as early as second grade having to stand up in front of the class for "show and tell." Show and tell is an opportunity for the student to teach the rest of the class something they may not already know or be aware of. Even young children can teach other children because everybody comes from a different background, culture, or upbringing. No two people know the same things. Over time and as the grades progress, this "show and tell" concept is carried on in the form of classroom presentations, book discussions, speeches, or assignments on a particular subject. Essentially, these are much the same as "show and tell": shared knowledge.

Although standing up in front of an entire classroom may be terrifying to some people (whether they are kids or grown-ups), the idea of presenting a topic to others obligates the presenter to share knowledge while giving the audience an opportunity to listen and learn something new. It's easy to regurgitate information or to memorize things. The challenge is in the ability to really *understand* those things, whether you are on the talking side or the listening end. The presenter fundamentally becomes the teacher of the topic he or she is presenting, thereby providing the audience with a depth of understanding of the subject.

This is why sharing is so important. By sharing the Dollar Code with others, we become presenters of the idea. We may be asked to explain what the Dollar Code is and how to use it. By engaging in conversations and communicating, we can come up with new ideas and become experts on the topics in which we share. We can come up with new tricks to save money and develop a true understanding of why spending money wisely is so important. These are yet more ways people can use the Dollar Code to positively impact their lives.

DOLLAR CODE **TIP #16**

"Share the Dollar Code concept with others to become an expert at doing it yourself. This will propel the positive impact and effectiveness it makes on your own life."

Developing a Support System

Starting something may be easy. People often start new things with great intentions, but then after a couple of weeks they just go back to their old ways. Joining the gym is a prime example. How many of those New Year's resolutions ever come to fruition? People have a habit of saying they will do something, and then as time goes on it just becomes less important. No matter how difficult or simple it may be, this is a character trait of many human beings.

Sticking to good intentions is not an easy task. Even though the Dollar Code is a simple concept and involves remembering only *one* number, we are all human. We may *know* how to use the Dollar Code, but then we run into those temptations. You know, the perfect Prada handbag that just went on clearance and might be gone by the end of the week, or the shiny new chrome rims for the car that we spot at the auto parts store and there just happens to be one set left. Everyone experiences temptations. That is exactly why people need a support system.

Think of all the greatest organizations worldwide that have stood the test of time. They all have support systems in place: Weight Watchers provides support for people who have a propensity for being overweight. Alcoholics Anonymous has a support system for people who suffer from an addiction to drinking or drugs. Schools have a support system called the PTA for parents, teachers, and administrators to support their students and programs. These groups all have one common denominator: They all rely on their support systems for encouragement. They share knowledge and ideas and help one another get through those tough, tempting moments. They all gather to discuss new ideas for making a situation better. Instead of being isolated, people are part of a community.

Having a good support system makes one less likely to cave in to temptations. It's like having a bunch of soldiers who are fighting on your behalf, and it also makes you more accountable. After all, it would be much easier to give up on something if you have nobody to answer to. Like the person who cheats on his or her diet and has to answer to the scale during their weekly Weight Watchers weigh-ins, or the person who falls off the wagon and has a drink, even though they are part of AA, having a network of people who are counting on you to accomplish something can actually make people reconsider those temptations. We are all human and like to have people think highly of us.

Another positive attribute of a support system is that many minds gathered together can be more powerful than just the thoughts of one individual. By stating your goals and presenting them to others, it enables everyone to hear you and to add their own ideas. You are all good for each other in a sense because you can help each other through the ups and downs. Someone else might have different ideas than you—maybe they will be better or not something you would be interested in. Either way, it only makes you stronger when you listen to and actively participate in a support system.

A lot of people wouldn't consider the need for a support system when it comes to their finances. Perhaps that is because finances are such a personal matter. But then again, so is drug or alcohol addiction, food addiction, or even nonaddictive personal matters such as raising children and exercise groups. If you think about it, this is an erroneous way of thinking. You do not need to disclose your finances or even have a severe problem in order to use and apply the Dollar Code. Instead, you should consider the opportunity for support as more of a way to cheer each other on. One of the coolest things about the Dollar Code is that, although you share your DA with others, *you are in no way disclosing how much money you make or how much money you spend*! Because your income and expenses are wrapped up into one number (your DA), no one is able to figure out your income! There is no better way to share with others while, at the same time, keeping your personal information *confidential*!

Having a strong network of family and friends will make you try harder to stay on track and stick to your goals. Especially in the matters of finance and budgeting, many people lack the know-how and just fly by the seat of their pants every day because they don't know what else to do. This is why having support is instrumental; it allows you to discuss those tough moments and bounce ideas off someone else or to others within your group. Plus, you can be there for new people after you become good at doing the Dollar Code. It will make you feel empowered and in control of your money situation, rather than feeling like a victim or slave of your money.

If you are someone who is very independent and private, I would still encourage you to find at least another friend or two to offer support. Maybe you're not the type who would be interested in attending a group support-style setting and would rather just call someone else who you can confide in. That's okay, too. Support is simply assistance or backing. It is someone who can give you advice and who will listen to your advice when they need it. So, for example, if you have a question about the Dollar Code, you can talk to each other and state what worked for you and what didn't.

Building a Dollar Code Community

Since the Dollar Code is a relatively new concept, you may find that there are few people who know about it, at least for right now. That puts you in a position of becoming a *leader*. Why not become the "go to" person who tells others and who helps to bring this great concept to your own community? Surely you know that if it works for you and you feel the benefits of doing the Dollar Code, then it would be worthwhile to share with others. Once your bank account gets fatter or your debt becomes lower, it will make you feel really good inside. Don't you want to share that good feeling with others? How great would it feel to help others and have them look up to you?

There are so many people who are living above their means and strapped for money, broke, and barely getting by. You can become a great role model by building a Dollar Code community that helps people to understand just how beneficial the Dollar Code can be in rebuilding their financial stability. Better yet, you can also encourage schools to implement a class that teaches students about budgeting and then bring the Dollar Code concept with you to present to the class. That way people can learn at a much younger age the value of budget management, rather than waiting until their personal financial matters are in turmoil.

With the power of the Internet, more people than ever are online and connected to others from around the world. The Internet presents the possibility for strangers to become friends, no matter where they live. Truly our world is e-connected with the rapid advancements in technology. In the past, people used to phone one another or write letters to stay in touch. Today they text, email, or simply "like" a comment on a social networking site like Facebook.

Add Facebook into the mix. Facebook is a whole community in and of itself. At the moment it seems to be the biggest "support network" in the entire world. No matter what type of hobby or interest you have, you can find others who share in similar hobbies and interests. Think of how exciting this is, even though people take it for granted. I know I have met people that I never would have had the opportunity to know had it not been for the Internet. I am grateful for the many new friendships and tremendous support I have found there. Not only does the Internet help businesses to grow, it offers endless possibilities of support for all of my endeavors.

Since you are now a Dollar Code participant, you are welcome to join the Dollar Code community and meet other like-minded individuals who share in your challenges and who are committed to stick to the Dollar Code because they have seen the difference it has made to their financial well-being. With a newly launched website (*www.TheDollarCode.com*), a useful Dollar Code blog, and our social networking presences, you can participate as much or as little as you like. Oh and while we're talking about "likes," go online and "Like" our page on Facebook (*www.Facebook.com/ TheDollarCode*)!

Competing with the Dollar Code: The Ultimate Dollar Code Challenge!

"What in the heck is a Dollar Code competition?" you may ask. Well, just like any competition, such as *Survivor* on TV or even a simple board game, having a friendly competition does two things. First of all, it helps you stay on track because people have

a natural desire to win. Winners succeed; therefore, competing against other participants with similar goals gives you a greater chance to stay focused. You will be less likely to cheat because you do not want to be the one who loses!

Another benefit of competing is that it makes using the system *fun*. I don't know anyone who would say that monthly budgeting is fun, but those who challenge others make their own fun by setting milestones and exceeding even their own expectations.

Some may say that they don't wish to disclose their personal information and that a budget or personal finances is certainly something not to be shared with others. On the contrary, since the Dollar Code uses only *one* number that combines all of your income and expenses, no one will ever know how you arrived at your personal DA! That's right! In other words, all of your finances are wrapped up into one, easy-to-remember number that will be different for every individual. For some people it may be as low as 10, while for others it might be as high as 50. You never have to disclose how much you make or how much you spend.

If you choose to become part of the Dollar Code community and to embrace the use of a support system as we have discussed in this chapter, then by now you have already seen the benefits of using the Dollar Code within your own life. So let the Dollar Code competition begin! Here are some challenges you can propose to others:

- ♦ Who can raise their DA the most?
- ♦ Who can stick to their Dollar Code the longest?
- ♦ Whose DA has increased the most drastically?

♦ Who has the most unique story about how the Dollar Code has improved their personal situation?

♦ Who is in it to win it?

Why not create a Dollar Code challenge where everyone allocates $1 per day to the "Dollar Code Winner's Pot?" At the end of the month, the winner gets the money to splurge on whatever he or she desires! If there are ten of you in the group, that's $300 for the winner!

After reading this chapter, you may decide that instead of relying on others for support and encouragement you would prefer to do the Dollar Code on your own, at least initially. That is fine. To paraphrase singer Bobby Brown, "*It's your prerogative.*" My wish for you is that no matter whether you go at the Dollar Code solo or whether you need the help of friends, family, or the Dollar Code community, you stick to the Dollar Code system. I am confident of its ability to transform your personal finances within a short period of time.

10 The Dollar Code for Entrepreneurs

S o far in this book as we have introduced and explained the Dollar Code concept, most of the talk has been about having a steady paycheck and a monthly income that you can rely on. Of course, for the majority of the people who are employees of a company, this would be seemingly easy to figure out, since you probably have a paycheck stub and a set salary or hourly rate that doesn't fluctuate very often.

However, many people do not have a steady paycheck because they are *self-employed*. As I have my own consulting firm, I can relate to these business owners because I have experienced the highs and lows of having an unstable income. In fact, I often work with many clients who are business owners. Self-employed people can be either individuals who work as freelancers, consultants, or as DBAs (doing business as), but they can also be people who own a company that employs a staff of workers and who operate as an LLC or other incorporation.

Because of this income instability, I am often asked by many entrepreneurs if the Dollar Code can be applied to businesses as well. The answer is . . . *of course!* If you've taken the plunge and quit your job to launch your own business, let me first say, "Congratulations!"

Did you know that there are over 27.2 million small businesses in the United States as of 2008 (according to the U.S. Census Bureau), and that number is growing every day? And in Canada there are 2.4 million small businesses (according to Statistics Canada). Small business ownership is one of the toughest yet most rewarding things people can take on. Those who have the guts to pursue their passion and dreams by owning a business will have many struggles, yet the successes will be all that much sweeter.

Personally, I quit my day job and started my own consulting business ten years ago. It's been awesome! Now, I'm not saying it's always been easy. Owning your own business can be very challenging and involves a lot of risks. At times you feel like you work much harder than you ever did at your regular job. However, the rewards of owning your own business are many. *You* set your own hours. *You* hire the people you want to work with (your employees!). *You* benefit from many tax savings. Most important, as a business owner . . . *you* are in control!

If you currently own a business or are thinking of starting one, pick up my book *The Dollar Code for Business Owners*. I am providing a brief introduction here on how to use the Dollar Code for your business, since many of you who may be reading will wonder how to go about figuring out your Dollar Code DA. However, I will go into much more depth in *The Dollar Code for Business Owners* and would encourage you to splurge on this beneficial financial reading guide. Within its pages I have many tips for business owners and also share secrets on tax savings and tax benefits that the government does not want you to know! Plus, it's a tax write-off!

First of all, the Dollar Code principle for a business is the same as it is for an individual. Your Dollar Code still involves *one* number (your DA), and the calculation of that number involves Money In and Money Out. That's where the similarities end.

Money In

Money In for an individual through a traditional paycheck is usually called a "wage" or "salary." For a person, the money comes in the form of cash. Now, what I mean is that it is a *sure thing.* The cash I'm talking about may be in the form of a check, but it could also be a direct deposit to your bank account. The method by which you get paid doesn't matter. What *does* matter is that the money is available to be used by you immediately.

For a business, however, the money coming into the business is called "revenue." Money In from customers of a business can either be cash or it could be called an "accounts receivable." The difference between the two is that cash can be used immediately by the business, whereas an account receivable is not available for use by the business right away. The business records revenue whenever a service is performed or when a product is sold. The customer who used its service or purchased a product is responsible to pay the business for it. Until the customer actually pays for that service or product (via cash, credit card, check, or other method), the money to be received is called an account receivable. Businesses record this transaction to recognize the revenue from it. This is called "accrual" accounting.

In using the Dollar Code for a business, you should *not* include any accounts receivable items. Instead, a business owner can use the same six months of receipts of both income and expenses and tally the income from the Money In. Then an average can be used to determine the DA to use moving forward. There is a more in-depth explanation on this approach in the *Dollar Code for Business Owners*.

DOLLAR CODE **TIP #17**

"Entrepreneurs will use revenue instead of paycheck stubs to determine their DA. They should use a three-month average of money coming in to determine the amount of income earned."

Loans and credit cards are, in essence, "Money In" because they allow extra money over and above the cash an individual or business has to spend to be used. Individuals use loans or credit cards to purchase products or services for personal use. Businesses use loans and credit cards to purchase items or services that enable them to make a *profit*, which is the reason a business exists in the first place. If a business does not make a profit, it will not survive for long!

I strongly, strongly advise individuals to use loans only in situations that are considered necessities, for example: getting a mortgage to buy a house. I do not recommend using a credit card for *any* individual purchases, under any circumstances. Remember . . . cash is king! As we explained in previous chapters, credit cards not only get you into financial trouble, they can often make an item that you purchase far more expensive than its original price because of interest and penalties (if you pay late or go over your limit).

When calculating the Dollar Code for a business, loans can be considered, but the calculation depends on what the loan is used for. Also, loan repayments must be taken into consideration, thus reducing the DA. Again, if you are a business owner I would encourage you to read more about this in *Dollar Code for Business Owners*.

An investment in a business is considered Money In. Therefore, investors such as banks, private lenders, other businesses, individuals, and so forth give businesses money to enable a business to make a profit and grow. Of course, an investor expects a return on their investment (known as an ROI), whether it is monetary or "other." "Other" could come in the form of a percentage of the company, its profits, or any tangible assets.

However, in most cases, the ROI is expected to be received as a monetary amount. If a business receives an investment for operating expenses versus capital expenses, this is the amount to use when calculating the business's DA. If it is a one-time investment, the business must apply the timeline that it will use over the Dollar Code calculation.

Money Out and Employee Involvement

The Money Out principle to use when doing the Dollar Code calculation for businesses is the same as it is for individuals. Just like anyone else, the business has its own list of expenses that must be factored within the budget and that must be paid on a month-to-month basis. So really, the only difference between a business and individual in regard to the Dollar Code is the *income* (Money In), not the expenses (Money Out).

Although you should always use caution when talking to your employees about any kind of financial matters, there is no reason why you should not tell them about the Dollar Code. *Why?*

Well, as we talked about in the last chapter, it is important to surround yourself with a support system and tell others about the Dollar Code. By spreading the word about how simple it is to do and by sharing the concept, you can position yourself as a leader on the topic. Plus, teaching employees the principle of a Dollar Code helps them understand how the business spends money. By understanding how much the business is allowed to spend on a daily basis, the staff can better identify with the businesses needs and make the same commitment as the owner in order to adhere to the number that is set forth. By revealing the Dollar Code for the business, you can make sure the employees do not go over that daily limit in their spending and this is an excellent way to keep costs in check.

You see, the Dollar Code can be a valuable tool not only for individuals but for entrepreneurs, as well. Some business owners that I have mentioned this idea to have loved it so much that they made it a requirement for all of their employees to learn. Others used the Dollar Code as a tool to "trim the fat" in a company's expenses and even hold weekly or monthly meetings that reevaluate the number used for the company Dollar Code. After all, if a monthly checkup is in store for people's personal finances, then why wouldn't it also be important for a business? The stakes are high in either case, so it can be used as a valuable tool both for individuals and for entire entities.

Another idea is to create a community for your employees to participate in and compete against one another for their own personal Dollar Codes. To encourage participation, the business could offer rewards for those employees who excel and really take the Dollar Code "ball" and run with it. Rewards could be either monetary or in the form of a certificate or plaque. Just remember that positive reinforcement is a great way to instill positive values and build employee loyalty. Plus, employees will appreciate the valuable tool that knowing the Dollar Code will become in their own lives, and you may see a difference in their attitudes. When people are depressed about money or about personal problems, this carries through in their attitude at work. So if you teach them how to effectively manage their money so they are not suffering, don't you think you will see many uplifted spirits and happier employees? You bet!

DOLLAR CODE **TIP #18**

"If you don't yet own a business but are thinking of starting one, allocate part of the DA you've calculated for yourself toward your initial business investment!"

How to Calculate Your Initial Investment

If you've been thinking about starting your own business but don't know where to begin, the Dollar Code can help you in the matter of getting enough funds to pursue your dream. Many people who work for a company do so because they fear losing their steady paycheck or guaranteed income from a stable job. This is a valid concern. It would truly be gutsy and even kind of stupid to just quit your job unexpectedly one day without any kind of plan. For some people, having a business is a lifelong dream that never gets accomplished because they lack the resources to get it off the ground. It's very scary to start a business when you have no direction and are not sure where to find customers or are unsure if you will generate enough income to pay those necessary living expenses, such as rent, utilities, auto, groceries, and child care obligations.

Knowing how to use and apply the Dollar Code can set you on the path to business ownership if that is one of your goals and dreams. All you need to do is set aside part of your Dollar Code every single day until you finally have the needed funds. That sounds easy, doesn't it? Well it can be done, but first you need to have an approximation of the cost of your initial business endeavor. Depending on what type of business you want to do, this could be a lot or a little money that you will be saving. If the number is a lot, it may be best to focus first on paying off debts so that you can free up extra money to make your DA higher. That will leave you less strapped for cash on a day-to-day basis, as well as tackling a mountain that will never seem to get smaller. After the debt (or some of it, at least) is paid, then you can start focusing on your dream of business ownership.

Here are a number of ways in which you can figure out how much money it will require for your business startup:

- **Make a business startup checklist.** A checklist is like a grocery list and helps you get a real look at what you need instead of treating your business venture as just a fantasy that will never happen. Some things that you can include on the list might be the following:
  - Your business name, registration, and incorporation
  - A business plan and marketing strategy
  - Occupational licenses, permits, or zoning requirements
  - A rate card or price sheet for your services or products
  - A short list of absolute must-haves to get started, such as computer equipment, office furniture, software, and supplies
  - A special bank account to keep the business finances separate from your personal affairs

- **Research.** Whether you go online or to the library, or ask other business owners with similar ventures, you must do your homework before diving into any venture. You can look at similar business models either within your own state or province or even in other communities. Whether the business is entirely an online venture or if it requires office or retail space should also be a consideration. If you need a location to run the business, get out there and go look at places that you think would be ideal for the type of business you wish to launch. Write everything down and make these factors part of your business plan.

- **Network with other entrepreneurs.** If you're not sure how much it will cost to get your business up and running, you can also reach out to some of the many industry-related trade associations available online and within your community. There are support groups that are designed specifically for the purpose of exchanging ideas, and by networking you can get help from people who have already "been there, done that" and who are willing to give you advice. The Small Business Administration's (SBA) Development Center (*www.sba.gov*) is also a great place to go and has offices in nearly every state. Aside from offering free or inexpensive advice on everything from startup capital or preparing a business plan, the SBA also offers ongoing support and counseling, workshops, and information about how to obtain loans and grants.

- **Write down one-time costs and ongoing costs.** The startup of a business is the most expensive part of getting it going. After you've been running it for a while, things will begin to run smoothly, and with proper management you will begin to see a profit. Initially you will need to know what is necessary to launch. This is a different list from the one we just mentioned previously because it offers a more detailed overview of every little nit-picking thing. This could include expenses such as business cards, a storefront sign, a website, and so forth. Some things will fall into a category of "one time" expenses, while others will be something you must factor into your monthly business budget. Here is where to find a useful list you could use to get your brain thinking about all of the contingencies for your business: www.businessknow how.com/StartUp/startup.htm.

No one ever decides to start a business with the intention of failure. That's why so many people never pursue their dream of starting one in the first place. They are afraid to because statistically it is known to be a rough road. But ask most any business owner and they will tell you that the risk is worth it in the end because it is far more rewarding to do your own thing than to rely on someone else for a paycheck and to be a slave to a job. It takes dedication, motivation, ambition, and time.

If your idea is something that allows you to start out slowly, such as after working at your regular job or on weekends and in your spare time, you could try that approach to get your feet wet without the huge commitment. Look for tax advantages that can give you a break and be a little conservative with your estimating and planning. If your dream is to have your own business, then I say, "Go for it!" and never look back. It's better to be happy and passionate about what you do than miserable at a job that you don't enjoy.

11 The Family Plan

I f you've come this far, then obviously you are intrigued and ready to embrace the concept of the Dollar Code. I am as excited to help you as you are to get started. Throughout the contents of this book, I hope I have offered an adequate explanation and good analogies for you to see how simple and easy it will be to calculate and use your DA.

One thing we haven't talked about yet is the Dollar Code and your family. So far we have talked about it on an individual level, as well as discussing how business owners/entrepreneurs can figure out their DA. It's one thing to be able to calculate a DA for yourself, but what if you have a spouse and kids? That can put a bit of a twist on the number you are using, especially if your spouse is not on the same page and is not as eager to learn the system of daily budget control.

First, let me say that doing the Dollar Code together has many benefits on your relationship. One of the biggest reasons is the fact that money is an essential part of your relationship and can either keep you together or drive you apart. According to numerous studies, money is one of the primary causes of divorce. One study from the Utah State University found that couples who had disputes over money once a week or more were 30 percent more likely to get divorced. During a bad economy, this number can be even worse.

I hope this is not the case in your household, but if money is a problem, then I hope the Dollar Code can be a great solution to save your relationship! Now I am not in any way a marriage counselor, but do know that if you team up and tackle your financial problems together instead of arguing about individual spending habits, your marriage will probably see fewer disputes.

Sharing Your Dollar Code

The biggest question on people's minds when they are trying to figure out how to apply the Dollar Code to their *shared* expenses is "How do I figure out a daily total for both of us?" This is a very good question. Indeed, your Dollar Code calculation will be different than it would be if you were responsible for only your own budget.

Before we even begin, the biggest thing is "buy-in"—what I mean by this is that each partner/spouse agrees to do the Dollar Code together—as a team. You can still do it on your own, but it makes it much easier if each of you is committed to the Dollar Code way of life. It's the same as if you were on a diet or implementing healthy eating in your family. It is much easier to do it together!

From my research, I have found that most couples/families do one of the following:

1. Keep all of their money in a joint account
2. Share a joint account for family expenses but have their separate accounts for their own personal spending
3. Have completely separate accounts where each person takes care of certain bills each month

One Joint Account

If you, as a couple/family, put your paychecks into one account and use that same account for expenses, then calculating your family's DA is almost the same as calculating your own personal DA. The only difference is that you have to split this daily amount that you calculate. Now, in most cases, you would just split this daily amount equally between the two of you. For example, if your DA is $40, then splitting it equally would give you each $20 a day for spending money. Remember that this number does not include the amounts for expenses that you've included when calculating your DA, such as grocery and gas bills. The other option you have is to take your DA and split it based on what each of you feels you want or need to spend. For example, Troy and Joni have calculated their family DA (daily spending amount) at $40. If Troy and Joni decide *between the two of them* that Troy needs more spending money per month because he's addicted to Starbucks (note that I'm not advocating this type of spending!), then they could split it so that Troy has more to spend than Joni—Troy's DA could be $25 while Joni's would then be $15. The important thing here is that the daily total between the two of them adds to that same $40!

Shared Joint Account with Separate Personal Accounts

Many couples choose to have one account that is used to pay all of the combined family expenses, such as mortgage, rent, groceries, and so forth, and then have separate accounts for their personal spending. This works well for many couples, as they are jointly committed to the family costs but each partner still has the ability to spend some money personally as how they see fit. This method of using the Dollar Code to calculate each DA is more like an individual calculation; the only difference is that the money each partner puts into the "joint" account is treated like an expense when each person is calculating his or her DA. For example, let's say that Aaron and Angela have a joint account, and each of them also has their own separate account. Aaron is an electrician who makes $3,000 per month. Aaron likes to drive a fancy car, so his car payment is $500 per month and his insurance is $100 per month. Aaron also contributes $1,500 per month to the joint account. Angela is a journalist who makes $4,000 per month. She drives a basic car and pays a car payment of only $200 per month, with auto insurance of $80 per month. Angela contributes $2,000 to the joint account each month. This is how their Dollar Code calculations would look:

Aaron				
Monthly income				$3,000
Monthly expenses				
	Car payment		$ 500	
	Insurance		100	
	Joint account		1,500	
				$ 2,100
Net amount (income less expenses)				$ 900
Aaron's DA (Net amount ÷ 31)				$ 29
Angela				
Monthly income				$ 4,000
Monthly expenses				
	Car payment		$ 200	
	Insurance		70	
	Joint account		2,000	
				$ 2,270
Net amount (income less expenses)				$ 1,730
Angela's DA (Net amount ÷ 31)				$ 56

Aaron has $29 per day that he can spend and Angela has $56.

Something interesting to note is that if Aaron chose to drive a similar vehicle to Angela's, with similar payments, his DA would be $40! This shows how applying a Dollar Code lifestyle (i.e., taking out some of the unnecessary items, such as the fancier car) can really benefit you and increase your DA!

Separate Accounts for Each Partner

Some couples prefer to hold separate accounts and not put anything into a joint account. Family expenses (such as mortgage, rent, etc.) must then be allocated by each partner. For example, with Adam and Kristi, Adam pays the mortgage each month while Kristi pays the utility bills. In this case, each person calculates their DA separately just as they would on an individual basis, as there is no sharing of income or expenses! The trick here is to ensure that each person calculates their DA using the monthly expenses that they pay. In this case, Adam would put the mortgage payment into his Dollar Code calculation and Kristi would put the monthly utility bills into hers. It's that simple! As a reminder, each person should tally the past *six* months and use the month with the highest bills and expenses when determining their DA!

One thing I would like to suggest is having a joint savings account, regardless of how you handle your monthly bills or your other accounts. The reason for this is that it encourages saving together as a team (one unit) and makes it easier for each person to help the other stay on track with saving for the future—something I consider very important!

DOLLAR CODE **TIP #19**

"When calculating your Dollar Code as a couple, try to avoid any conflicts by being honest with each other about daily spending habits. By striving toward the same goal of getting ahead, you can both cut back where necessary and stick to your DA as a couple instead of individually. Together you can repair your finances and even save a strained relationship!"

Is There an App for That?

I have created a wonderful tool to help both individuals and couples with their dedication to the Dollar Code. It is an iPhone and Android application that allows to people to "share" their DA and can be updated daily. So, for example, let's say that you and your husband or wife have arrived at a DA of $48 for each day as a combined unit. That means each of you gets to spend only $24 dollars in order to stick to your Dollar Code budget.

The app can be used as a great tool for this very reason. Both the wife and husband can update their usage of the DA throughout the day and can go open the app to get a glimpse of how much is left. It's not really meant to be a tracking device to keep tabs on each other's DA; rather, it is designed to be a way for you both to stay focused on your goal of sticking to the budget.

My advice to couples is to use the Dollar Code as a way to communicate, to stay focused, and to be dedicated to your mutual goal of (1) getting out of debt, and (2) paying bills on time and managing money better. I have seen it work well, and when both people in the relationship are committed to making it work, it can save your relationship a lot of financial stress!

Dollar Code Dos and Don'ts for Couples

Because money is a common problem between two people, the need for having a system becomes even more important. The Dollar Code works if both people want to make it work. If one does it wholeheartedly but the other person often breaks the rules, it can cause more conflict than good. Ideally, both of you must be in agreement that you want to give it your best effort and really stick to the program.

Going back to the chapter we talked about with the emergency savings fund, I think it becomes even more important to get one if you have a family at stake. If one person loses their job or becomes unable to work due to an illness or other complication, the emergency savings fund can be a real lifesaver for a marriage. Let's go over a few more *dos,* . . . and while we're at it we'll also mention some *don'ts:*

Do . . .

- ✔ Set up and add to an emergency fund in the form of a savings account, either individually or jointly.

- ✔ Talk with your partner about your financial goals and strategy for getting out of debt or acquiring wealth.

- ✔ Learn how to use and apply the Dollar Code together so that you are both striving to reach the same goals.

Don't . . .

- ✔ Ignore bills until the last minute. Late fees and penalties are very costly and can blow your budget out of the water.

- ✔ Justify tomorrow to buy today by using credit cards that only rack up more debt. For that matter, try to avoid loans for "play toys," such as four-wheelers, boats, motorcycles, or splurges that can get your family in too much debt. Pay cash for these items if you have the means to do so!

- ✔ Write a check for a bill or purchase until you have actually deposited the money into your account. Late fees and floating checks can be very costly and banks charge anywhere between $29 to $39 for every insufficient funds transaction.

- ✔ Set up automatic payments unless you are certain of the funds being available. These auto payments can be a love/hate relationship if they cross paths, and banks often find a way to sock it to you if they happen to deduct the automatic payment before your paycheck or direct deposit actually hits your bank account.

How Using the Dollar Code
Has Changed Lives

Head over to the Dollar Code website (*www.TheDollarCode .com*) to see how the Dollar Code has changed people's lives. On our website, we also have more tips and tricks for your Dollar Code lifestyle!

DOLLAR CODE **TIP #20**

"You can do it! Set aside some uninterrupted time to calculate your Dollar Code at the start. Each day, use the 5-Minute Checkup to stay on track. Keep your DA in your head, and soon your stress levels about money will decrease and you'll be on your way to financial freedom!"

12 A Twenty-Tip Recap

The best part about incorporating the Dollar Code into your own life is that it doesn't ask you to give up things. Some books will tell you that you *must* buy cheaper, generic items instead of name brand items or to quit drinking your daily cup of java that you love and yearn for every day. The Dollar Code is a much easier and more effective budgeting approach because, instead of having to give up the things you crave or love, it teaches you how to stay within a budget for that day and find a balance. In a sense, it encourages better decision making, and that is certainly never a bad thing.

Remember when you were a kid and you didn't have a real job like your parents did? Maybe they gave you an allowance or maybe you were fortunate enough to earn money in other ways, such as mowing lawns or selling lemonade or other common "kid things" to make money. Do you remember what it felt like when you finally did have some money in your hands? It was special. It was rewarding. It was awesome and made you feel like a grownup.

However, most of the time the amount of money you earned, acquired, or obtained was not a large sum. It may have been enough to go buy a toy, game, or some candy that you really wanted. And if there was something really *big* that you wanted but didn't have enough money yet to buy it, then maybe you were one of those kids who saved your money to get that thing once you finally earned enough to do so. That was something that forced you to be responsible with your money because it was much more difficult to come by than as an adult.

Adults have too many opportunities to overspend because they can get credit cards, loans, and other dangerous things. The Dollar Code is almost a childlike concept in its simplicity, and that is exactly why it works so well. It brings you back to a time when your parents gave you an "allowance." If you didn't have enough money, you certainly couldn't spend it. The Dollar Code is a very similar premise.

That is exactly how you should treat the DA that you come up with. You should get up every day, knowing that you cannot spend more than your allowance, and you can even pretend you don't have it to spend. Just like a kid, you can choose to save some of it for something bigger and better, or you can waste it frivolously. The choice is yours. In fact, leave those credit cards behind and just pretend they don't exist. You will see a noticeable difference in your financial well-being within only a few weeks if you adopt this mind-set.

Summary of Tips
for Dollar Code Diehards

Throughout the book, you may have noticed some "bold" ideas in the gray boxes. Those represent special tips that illustrate or highlight the concept that is being discussed within each chapter. Because I like to make your life easier, I am putting all of these wonderful tips here for you as a recap. This should make it even easier to follow along.

DOLLAR CODE **TIP #1**

"Having a system that is easy to use and easy to remember will help you stick to that system."

DOLLAR CODE **TIP #2**

"Kids learn about spending habits from parents because personal financial responsibility is not something taught in school. If you live in debt, your kids are likely to follow suit."

DOLLAR CODE **TIP #3**

"Being an adult who spends on impulse is no different than being a kid who gets a weekly allowance and then spends it all at once on candy or toys. Both are examples of financial mismanagement."

DOLLAR CODE **TIP #4**

"Learn to think about your spending on a daily basis, rather than at the end of the month. Budgeting on a monthly basis is too overwhelming."

DOLLAR CODE **TIP #5**

"Your Dollar Code is made up of two components: your income and your expenses. Look at your total monthly take-home pay. Then add up all the recurring bills and living expenses that you are committed to. Then divide this by 31."

DOLLAR CODE **TIP #6**

"Start eliminating things that set you back, things you don't need, or packages that are too big. Communications can be a tremendous money waster for many families."

DOLLAR CODE **TIP #7**

"Treat yourself enough but not too often. That way it will mean something."

DOLLAR CODE **TIP #8**

"Think about your impulse buying. It is often the smaller items that will eat you alive. Be conscious of spending habits and decisions."

DOLLAR CODE **TIP #9**

"Always recalculate your DA as soon as possible if you experience any changes to your income or recurring bills."

DOLLAR CODE **TIP #10**

"To avoid impulse buying, put your purchase off for a day. If you've forgotten about it or it seems

less important, you didn't really need it in the first place."

DOLLAR CODE **TIP #11**

"Make it inconvenient to have access to your own savings account. Having to withdraw it at the bank will deter you from impulsively taking it out to use on spontaneous items."

DOLLAR CODE **TIP #12**

"When looking at your three-month period, use the lowest amount of pay and the highest bill amounts."

DOLLAR CODE **TIP #13**

"Although it doesn't matter which method of payment you use to apply to your DA, cash should always be your top choice."

DOLLAR CODE **TIP #14**

"In order to keep track of your DA in your head, simply deduct every purchase as you go about your day."

DOLLAR CODE **TIP #15**

"Whenever there is change involved in your purchase, round it up to the higher number. So $6.39 becomes $7. This is another method to keep you from going over."

DOLLAR CODE **TIP #16**

"Share the Dollar Code concept with others to become an expert at doing it yourself. This will propel the positive impact and effectiveness it makes on your own life."

DOLLAR CODE **TIP #17**

"Entrepreneurs will use revenue instead of paycheck stubs to determine their DA. They should use a three-month average of money coming in to determine the amount of income earned."

DOLLAR CODE **TIP #18**

"If you don't yet own a business but are thinking of starting one, allocate part of the DA you've calculated for yourself toward your initial business investment!"

DOLLAR CODE **TIP #19**

"When calculating your Dollar Code as a couple, try to avoid any conflicts by being honest with each other about daily spending habits. By striving toward the same goal of getting ahead, you can both cut back where necessary and stick to your DA as a couple instead of individually. Together you can repair your finances and even save a strained relationship!"

DOLLAR CODE **TIP #20**

"You can do it! Set aside some uninterrupted time to calculate your Dollar Code at the start. Each day, use the 5-Minute Checkup to stay on track. Keep your DA in your head, and soon your stress levels about money will decrease and you'll be on your way to financial freedom!"

These tips can help you make learning and using the Dollar Code even more beneficial. I would encourage you to give this easy system a try whether you make a little or a lot of money. The Dollar Code is not just for the poor or rich. It is a tool for anyone who wants to succeed with an easy-to-apply budget. Once you get good at doing it, you will swear by its effectiveness in your own life. After all, you have to remember only ONE number. Going about your day in the same way you ever have, you can keep this number at the forefront of your thoughts to make better decisions with regard to your finances. Before you know it, your debt will shrink and your bank account will grow. So will your DA!

The Dollar Code Worksheet

	Amounts	(convert to monthly)

Sources of Income

Income source 1	_____	1
Income source 2	_____	2
Income source 3		3
Total Money In	$ _____	Sum (1 to 3)

Monthly Savings

Debt reduction	_____	10
Car repair acct	_____	11
Home reno acct	_____	12
Vacation acct	_____	13
Emergency Fund	_____	14
401k 1	_____	15
401k 2	_____	16
Other	_____	17
A	_____	Sum (10 to 17)

Monthly Expenses
Home

Mortgage	_____	20
Property Taxes	_____	21
Condo Fees	_____	22
Insurance	_____	23
Gas	_____	24
Electricity	_____	25
Alarm system	_____	26
Phone	_____	27
Internet, cable TV	_____	28
Cleaner	_____	29
Yard maintenance	_____	30
Other		31
B	_____	Sum (20 to 31)

Car

Car payment   _____ 40
Gas   _____ 41
Insurance   _____ 42
Registration   43

C [_____] **Sum (40 to 43)**

Banking, Interest, and Insurance

Checking 1   _____ 50
Checking 2   _____ 51
VISA interest   _____ 52
Line of credit payment   _____ 53
Health insurance   _____ 54
Travel insurance   _____ 55
Other   56

D [_____] **Sum (50 to 56)**

Health & Beauty

Groceries   _____ 60
Dry cleaning   _____ 61
Gym membership   _____ 62
Other memberships   _____ 63
Clothing club   _____ 64
Haircut   _____ 65
Manicure/Pedicure   _____ 66
Cosmetics   _____ 67
Pilates   _____ 68
Physio   _____ 69
Massage   _____ 70
Facial   _____ 71
Other   72

E [_____] **Sum (60 to 72)**

Business/Admin

Cell phone   _____ 80
Parking   _____ 81
Subscriptions   _____ 82
Other   83

F [_____] **Sum (80 to 83)**

Memberships

Membership 1	_____	90
Membership 2	_____	91
Membership 3	_____	92
G		**Sum (90 to 92)**

Giving Back

Donation 1	_____	100
Donation 2	_____	101
Donation 3	_____	102
Donation 4	_____	103
Misc		104
H		**Sum (100 to 104)**

Periodic Expenses (you must convert to monthly)

Car maintenance	_____	110
School fees	_____	111
Other		112
I		**Sum (110 to 112)**

Total Money Out $ _____ (Sum A to I)

Write down your
Money In amount _____ (a)

Write down your
Money Out amount _____ (b)

Subtract the two amounts _____ (a) – (b)

Divide that number by 31 ÷ **31**

Your DA $ _____